# Schools of Quality: An Introduction to Total Quality Management in Education

Dedicated to
Walter A. Shewhart
Who Started It All

# Schools of Quality

## An Introduction to Total Quality Management in Education

John Jay Bonstingl

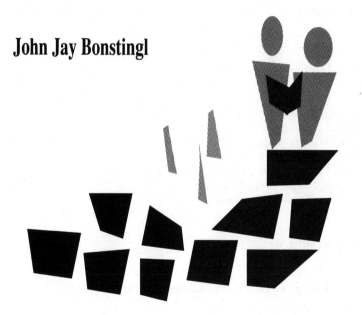

![ASCD]

Association for Supervision
and Curriculum Development

Association for Supervision and Curriculum Development
1250 N. Pitt St.
Alexandria, VA 22314
(703) 549-9110

Printed in the United States of America.

Ronald S. Brandt, *Executive Editor*
Nancy Modrak, *Managing Editor, Books*
Ginger R. Miller, *Associate Editor*
Jennifer L. Beun, *Assistant Editor*
Gary Bloom, *Manager, Design and Production Services*
Karen Monaco, *Senior Graphic Designer*
Valerie Sprague, *Desktop Typesetter*

ASCD Stock Number: 611-92152

**Library of Congress Cataloging-in-Publication Data**

Bonstingl, John Jay.
    Schools of quality : an introduction to total quality management
in education / John Jay Bonstingl.
      p.    cm.
    Includes bibliographical references (p.    ).
    ISBN 0-87120-202-6 : $14.95
    1. School management and organization—United States.
    2. Total quality management—United States.  3. Teaching.  I. Title.
    LB2805.B65    1992
    371.2'00973—dc20
                                             92-35307
                                               CIP

# How to Use This Book

Welcome to the world of Total Quality Management! I wrote this book as a guide to help you think through the basic ideas of Total Quality Management in education. It is not meant to be a comprehensive guidebook or handbook, but rather an accessible introduction to a rather complex but highly important philosophy.

In this book you'll learn (or rediscover) the history of the Total Quality movement in Japan and the United States. We'll explore some aspects of TQM's philosophical and cultural foundations, and see how educators are using TQM principles and practices to improve all aspects of schooling from teacher training to school systems and community groups to teachers and students in classrooms.

This book is meant not just to be read, but to be *used!* Please interact freely with the ideas in this book. Scribble your thoughts, feelings, sketches, diagrams—whatever comes to mind—in the margins.

Certainly, this entire book can be read in a very short time. But it may prove more beneficial as you read for you to stop and reflect on the ways the ideas presented here might be helpful as you devise your own processes for the transformation of education.

This book reflects some of the most important aspects of TQM, which is based on the conviction that sharing a personal constancy of purpose and a dedication to continuous improvement are required for any meaningful change to take root. So as you read this book, consider how you can best embark on a journey of continuous improvement of yourself and the persons and processes around you, in your work with students and fellow educators, at home with your family, and in your community.

# 1

## The Bell Curve Meets *Kaizen*

Not long ago, I conducted an inservice seminar for teachers who were using a textbook I had authored. One of the teachers stayed behind to talk with me after the seminar. His red coach's jacket was inscribed with the name "Bob."

"Jay," he began solemnly, "I want to tell you something about your book."

"Please tell me," I responded.

"Well, I've really enjoyed teaching with it. The kids love it, too, and I get high marks from their parents. But I'm having one big problem with that textbook of yours." Bob showed a hint of a smile.

"Really? Tell me about it," I replied.

His expression became stern again.

"In the four years I've used your book for my course, none of my students has ever made lower than a B, and I don't give away grades."

I'm sure my face showed my delight.

"Well, congratulations, Bob! That's quite a success story. All of your students are succeeding in the learning process, and they're enjoying it! That's terrific! You must be very proud!"

He shook his head slowly. I was baffled.

"So, Bob, what's the problem?"

"My kids are all getting high grades, and they're all enjoying the course. *That's the problem!* My administrators think my course is worthless unless a sizeable percentage of my students are making C's, D's, and failing grades! I guess we're *too* successful!"

Bob then took out some of his students' work to assure me that his standards were very high. It was some of the best student work I had ever seen, demonstrating a variety of fresh perspectives expressed with creativity, self-confidence, and enthusiasm.

"This is great stuff!" I exclaimed.

Bob sighed and looked away, a flash of anger crossing his face. "None of that work deserves a C," he said, "and certainly not anything lower."

I agreed.

"Bob, is this what we're really talking about?" I picked up a piece of chalk and drew a bell-shaped curve on the board.

Bob nodded. "That's it! My administrators think that a bell curve is the ideal result of good work. Dumb, isn't it?"

Dumb, maybe. But this conception of educational success has been around for a long time. I thought about all the times I had heard teachers and administrators from every region of the country refer to this philosophy. In fact, the bell curve was a fundamental tenet of the education courses I took in college, modeled by my cooperating teacher in the student teaching experience, and confirmed by standard practice thereafter in every secondary school in which I taught.

I thought of the contrasting views of success I have heard over the years from elementary and high school teachers who participated in the graduate education classes I teach.

I always enjoy asking them the question: "How do you know when you're successful in your teaching?" Almost invariably, elementary school teachers tell me that they know they are most successful when their students are all continuously improving and feeling good about themselves and their new learnings.

What a contrast with the answer many high school teachers give to the same question! "My course has real meat to it," one Advanced Placement history teacher beamed. "Very few students have ever gotten an A in *my* class."

A college professor I had in a seminar for German majors had put it similarly many years ago as he explained his grading policy on the first day of class: "A's are for *Gott*," he declared, pointing to the heavens. "B's are for scholars such as myself," he proclaimed with an open hand pointing at his chest. He paused for a deep breath. "C's, D's, and E's are for you," he said with his right arm sweeping across the classroom, as he consigned all of us to the depths of mediocrity and worse.

Why does it seem that the farther we get from 1st grade, the less likely we are to view education's central purpose as nurturing people's innate potential through the development of patterns of success, and the more likely we are to view education as a judgmental, gatekeeping function?

Bob's voice broke my reverie. "Jay, what can I tell my administrators so they understand where I'm coming from?"

I thought for a moment. Bob's coach's jacket provided me with an insight.

"You're a football coach, right?"

He nodded.

"Okay, take a look at this line of scrimmage." I drew on the board:

**7**

**3**        **9**

**6**

**1**  **2**  **4**  **5**  **8**  **10**  **11**

"If we were to create a bell curve for your team," I suggested, "might it look like this?" I continued my drawing, superimposing a bell curve over the players' positions.

"Okay, let's say player #11 is terrific—a real all-star." He does everything right. Player #1, on the other hand, has absolutely no understanding of the game. He can't even move. His feet might as well be cemented to the ground."

Bob offered to continue my metaphor: "Players #2 and #3 aren't much better, but players #9 and #10 are very good—not as good as #11, but still very good."

"Players #4, #5, #6, #7, and #8," Bob continued, "are only average. And just look at the positions they are playing—the most important positions on the team!"

Bob stopped to think about what he had just said. "No, actually that's not right. *Each* of those positions is important. The team works like a system. If all of the system's parts are working together successfully, we do well. But if any part of the system shows any weakness, you can bet the opposing team will capitalize on it."

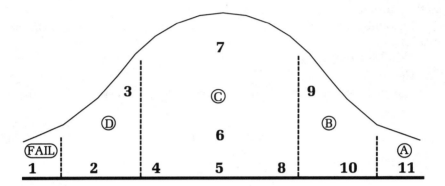

"Okay, Coach," I said, pointing to the bell-curved football team on the board, "what kind of a season do you think this team is going to have?"

Bob chuckled. "I wouldn't want to coach that team, Jay. It's going to be a long season for them!"

Bob then shared one of his "success secrets" with me. "When things are really clicking in my classroom, it's a lot like a championship football team playing on the field. There's a kind of electricity in the air. Everybody is psyched up and they are all helping each other, making sure that everybody on the team is successful. There's a special *synergy*— everybody feeding on one another's enthusiasm and dedication and sharp focus. It's an amazing sight!"

Bob thought silently for a moment, then said, "Why can't our schools be like that?"

Why, indeed!

I shared with Bob another analogy. "What might happen if, today, all the chief executive officers of all the businesses in the United States—from Exxon and General Motors down to the smallest mom-and-pop stores—sat down at one huge conference table and agreed that from this day forward they would all, *by design*, make sure that every day's products and services conform to the bell-shaped curve? Some of their output would be good or even excellent, but most would be mediocre or inferior. How long would such businesses survive in today's highly competitive global marketplace?"

"But," Bob retorted, "even the harshest critics of American education wouldn't suggest that we deliberately design mediocrity and failure into the work we do with kids in schools, would they?"

Maybe not. But ask children who have been in school for a few years, and you will find that almost all of them know in which of the five pigeonholes of the bell curve they belong. One bright 4th grade girl once told me, with a weary voice, that she never was good in math and that she would probably always get low grades in that subject. Early academic failures tend to be self-fulfilling prophesies for later years. Young people who grow up believing that, despite their best efforts, they are incapable of achieving quality results in their schoolwork, begin to see *themselves* as having little inherent quality. Rightly or wrongly, they may even come to believe that schools exist, not to help them improve, but rather to judge, criticize, and rank-order their efforts.

Today, a philosophy called Total Quality and its practice, called Total Quality Management (TQM), are helping educators view themselves as supporters rather than judges, as mentors and coaches rather than lecturers, as partners with parents, students, administrators, teachers, businesses, and entire communities rather than isolated workers within the walls of the classroom. We now understand that the only way we can ensure our own growth is by helping others to grow; the only way to maximize our own potentials is by helping others to improve little by little, day by day. The Japanese call this personal dedication to mutual improvement kaizen. The deeply ingrained ethos of kaizen lies at the heart of Japan's miraculous postwar revival. It is also the heart and soul of Total Quality. In this book we explore the new world of TQM, from its American origins in this century to its abrogation by American industry and its adoption (through the efforts of American statistical consultants) by major Japanese industries and the entire Japanese society.

Hundreds of schools and communities are now beginning to explore ways of adopting Total Quality as an operational norm. The people of these schools and communities are in the process of transforming their thoughts and lifestyles to mirror the crucial decision they have made to dedicate their efforts to continuous self-improvement and to the continuous improvement of the people with whom they live, work, and study.

The principles and practices of Total Quality Management have much to teach educators, as we join in the struggle to transform our entire society from a "Nation at Risk" into a Nation of Quality.

# 2

# Quality Comes (Back) to America

Remember when the words "Made in Japan" were the cause of laughter, scorn, and derision? Before and shortly after World War II, Japanese products were widely regarded—and with good reason—as cheap, poorly made, and easily destructible. On his television show, Jack Benny poked fun at Japanese manufacturing quality by wearing an inexpensive, new "Japanese" suit that came apart, piece by piece, during his monologue. The audience roared with laughter, acknowledging the essential truth not only of Benny's vaunted frugality, but also of the widely held public perception of Japanese goods.

Modern-day Japan, by contrast, is one of the world's great economic and industrial powers. "Made in Japan" is now considered the emblem of highest quality in virtually every type of item Japan exports. Japanese industrial and government leaders credit Japan's dramatic postwar turnaround in great part to a small group of Americans, including W. Edwards Deming and Joseph M. Juran, who taught Japanese industrialists the principles of Statistical Process Control (SPC), a methodology for consistently producing high-quality goods and services.

Today, the watchword of successful persons, businesses, schools, and other organizations worldwide is "Quality." Our understanding of Total Quality and its implications for education will depend upon an understanding of TQM's development in the United States and the Americans who developed it.

# The Beginning of the Total Quality Concept

William Edwards Deming was born on October 14, 1900, and earned his Ph.D. in physics at Yale in 1927. As a graduate student in the late 1920s, Deming worked summer jobs in Chicago at Western Electric's Hawthorne plant, the site of later experiments by Harvard researcher Elton Mayo on the correlations between the work environment, employee motivation, and productivity.

At Hawthorne, Deming observed the sweatshop conditions under which the predominantly female workforce of 46,000 labored to produce telephone equipment. The Hawthorne plant, like many other production facilities in the early 20th century industrialized world, operated under the philosophy of "scientific management" popularized by Frederick Winslow Taylor, an American industrial engineer. Taylor taught industrialists that workers should be hired to perform a small number of tasks in a repetitive, mechanistic fashion. They should not be hired to think about the work they do because thinking was the rightful role of management. Factory owners, according to Taylor, were to plan the work process and hire managers who would direct the workers. Workers, largely uneducated and untrained for the job, were urged by their bosses to continuously "work harder" and "do their best."

Scientific management principles discouraged workers from considering ways they could work more effectively and efficiently. Workers would surely make mistakes, but the inspectors at the end of the production line could catch faulty products before they left the plant, and workers' per-piece pay could be lowered for each item that had to be scrapped or reworked. If a worker produced too many faulty items, he or she could be dismissed.

Taylor's scientific management philosophy viewed the entire production process mechanistically. Equipment was designed to be interchangeable and easily replaceable, and workers were thought about in similar terms. Taylor taught American industry to view every line worker as "a cog in the giant industrial machine, whose job could be defined and directed by appropriately educated managers, administering a set of rules" (Walton 1991). Tasks on the assembly line were simple, repetitive, and boring. Workers' compliance with management's dictates was ensured by the hierarchical, top-down paradigm reminiscent of the turn-of-the-century Prussian army. In line with Taylor's model, workers at the Hawthorne plant were paid according to the number of pieces they produced per day. Higher output meant higher take-home pay. Quality of work was not a consideration for most workers. Inspectors at the end of the production line were entrusted with quality control, to the extent that product quality was an issue.

This philosophy of management was well-suited to the new assembly-line processes developed by Henry Ford and copied widely in America's private and public sectors. Taylor's philosophy made it possible for waves of immigrants, many of whom could not read, write, speak English, or oftentimes even communicate with one another, to find employment in American factories. Taylor's ideas soon found their ways into the nation's schools. The turn-of-the-century mass education movement took as its model the American factory, complete with the philosophy of Scientific Management. Franklin Bobbitt of the University of Chicago "took on the role of translating Frederick Taylor's principles . . . into a form in which they could be used by educators." He, like Taylor, believed that

> efficiency depended on the 'centralization of authority and definite direction by the supervisors of all processes performed . . . . The worker [that is, the teacher] . . . must be kept supplied with the detailed instructions as to the work to be done, the standards to be reached, the methods to be employed, and the appliances to be used . . . .' The results of the work of the planning department had to be 'transmitted to the teachers so that there can never be any misunderstanding as to what is expected of a teacher in the way of results or in the matter of method. This means that instruction must be given as to everything that is to be done' (Callahan from Marshall and Tucker 1992).

At the Hawthorne Plant, Deming became convinced that the authoritarian Taylor method of management was degrading to the human spirit and counterproductive to the interests of employees, management, and the company.

At Bell Laboratories in New Jersey, Deming met Walter A. Shewhart, a statistician who was leading the company's efforts to improve the reliability of telephones. Shewhart's goal was to make phones so well that the American phrase "as alike as two peas" would be replaced by "as alike as two telephones" (Kilian 1992). Toward this goal, Shewhart developed a methodology for improving worker performance and production output by measuring the extent to which the items produced fell within acceptable limits of variation. Shewhart developed a way of showing this variation graphically, which he called a statistical control chart. He shared his findings with Deming, his young protégé.

Deming recognized that, with training, workers could keep control charts of their own work and thus monitor the quality of the items they sent down the production line. Deming believed that if workers could be educated and empowered to manage their own work processes, the quality of their output would improve and the costly and ineffective end-of-line inspection process could be curtailed or eliminated. High quality would cost less, not more.

Shewhart also showed Deming a three-step cyclical process to help ensure increasingly higher quality production. Shewhart's cycle of Specification-Production-Inspection focused attention on inspection as the genesis of revised specifications, rather than as an end-of-line failsafe mechanism.

Deming later modified this three-step cycle into a four-step process, now commonly known as the Deming Cycle or the PDSA Cycle (although Deming has always referred to it as the Shewhart Cycle in honor of his mentor).

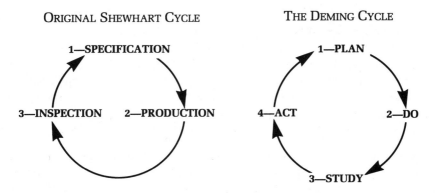

ORIGINAL SHEWHART CYCLE

1—SPECIFICATION

3—INSPECTION    2—PRODUCTION

THE DEMING CYCLE

1—PLAN

4—ACT    2—DO

3—STUDY

The Deming Cycle (Plan-Do-Study-Act)[1], like Shewhart's earlier model, is cyclical: First, a production plan is created. Then the plan is implemented on a small scale. In the third stage, production is studied

___

[1]Deming's PDSA Cycle was originally known as the PDCA Cycle, with "check" in place of "study."

to make sure it conforms to the plan. Finally, lessons learned in the study stage are used to modify the ongoing production process so that a new set of data can be used in creating and implementing the next plan, on a larger scale. Thus, the PDSA Cycle is a simple, effective, data-driven instrument for continuous learning and improvement.

Shewhart's discoveries and teachings became the centerpiece of Deming's emerging philosophy of Quality Management, which he taught first to Americans, then to the vanquished Japanese. During World War II, Deming was called by the U.S. government to support the war effort. As David Halberstam (1986) recounts, the War Department, impressed by Shewhart's work, brought together a small group of experts on statistical process control to help establish quality guidelines for defense contractors. Deming was part of that group, and he "came to love the work, for it concerned itself not just with mathematical excellence but with social value as well, helping people to make their products better and thus to make lives better" (Halberstam 1986).

Using Deming's application of Shewhart's ideas in the war effort, American manufacturers were able to produce superior military equipment. Japanese engineers studying captured American planes realized by 1942 that Japan's military fortunes were doomed.

> As they examined captured material they were sickeningly aware that the Americans were turning out better-made machines—machines that were obviously mass-produced—and that Japanese pilots were being sent into the skies hopelessly mismatched. Even in the postwar years, the Japanese were embarrassed by the shoddiness of their goods. If it rained in Tokyo, ten thousand phones might be out of order (Halberstam 1986).

At the war's end, American industry converted to peacetime production of goods and services for a voracious, affluent American public and worked to satisfy consumers' material needs and wants worldwide. As beneficiaries of the only industrialized economy left unscathed by the war, American industry could hardly keep up with demand. In the rush to satisfy consumer demand, American manufacturers focused on increasing production, leaving behind the quest for ever-increasing quality. Deming's frustration grew. He saw mounting evidence of America's abandonment of his and Shewhart's work. "Nothing was left of it, not even dust," said Deming (Deming seminar 1992).

And yet, in the late 1940s, many American manufacturers boasted about the quality built into their products. Companies such as Ford spoke with pride about the personal attention their workers gave to every aspect of production. *The Quality Revolution* (1989) shows a clip of a 1949 promotional film with a family climbing into their new Ford convertible at a dealer's showroom and driving home, as the announcer's voice says of the new owners: "As the road unfolds under their air-cushioned wheels, they are not quite alone." Each car carries "something of the designers who took ideas and put them on paper, something of the tool-and-die men, the core makers, the girls who lubricated the steel sheets when they went into the press. The skills, the heart they put into their work rides with this car always!"

Ironically, over the next 30 years, the decline of the American car industry came to symbolize our national industrial demise. Billions of dollars and a huge chunk of the international market were lost to German and Japanese competitors, phoenixes risen from the ashes of war. American economic and industrial might dwindled in the face of global competition. American workers grew more and more disaffected, less caring about the quality of their work, and increasingly convinced that employers no longer cared about them and their families. Color TVs, VCRs, and other high-tech products invented in the postwar United States were made by willing and increasingly able manufacturers in Japan, Korea, and other countries, where business leaders readily learned the lessons of quality that the United States had seemingly forgotten.

In truth, Japanese industry had begun to apply statistical methodologies before the war, but had abandoned their efforts when the war began (Gabor 1990). Then, in 1946, a group of leading industrialists created a new organization, the Union of Japanese Scientists and Engineers (JUSE), to advance the cause of quality Japanese manufacturing. Japan's desperate straits were evident everywhere. There were precious few indigenous resources, a terrible housing shortage, and very little food. Japan could not afford to continue exporting junk. Only high-quality exports could bring Japan the hard currency required to import the food necessary to keep the Japanese people from starving in their devastated postwar environment.

In 1949, Deming was asked by the State Department to go to Japan to help that government prepare for the 1951 census because of the work Deming had done for the U.S. Census Bureau in the late 1940s. The Japanese government needed statistical population studies to know how desperate the housing shortages were, and how best to remedy the situation.

While in Japan, Deming met with his fellow statisticians. They had known for several years about Shewhart's work from handwritten, mimeographed translations of his writings. And many of them had attended a series of lectures on statistical process control sponsored by the Civil Communications Section (CCS) of the Allied command. The lectures were presented by three American quality control experts who had worked for Bell Labs and Western Electric. They stressed the importance of preventing mistakes before they happen rather than fixing them after the fact. High quality costs less, not more, they preached. They taught that high-quality supplies are required to make high-quality products.[2]

# Total Quality in Japan

In 1950, JUSE, with the blessings of General Douglas MacArthur's office, invited Deming back to Japan to give a series of lectures on statistical quality control. MacArthur had his own good reasons for welcoming Deming's return. The Supreme Allied Commander wanted to communicate directly by radio with the Japanese people throughout the country. Japanese radios, however, were at the time highly unreliable. Deming, it was reasoned, could show the Japanese how to use statistical process control to make durable, reliable radios, which the Occupation Forces could place in at least 50 percent of all homes in Japan.

In his JUSE-sponsored lectures, Deming taught his Japanese audience how to use the Deming (PDSA) Cycle to constantly improve quality, and demonstrated the use of the statistical control charts pioneered by Shewhart, all of which he had done earlier for audiences in the United States. In *The Deming Management Method*, Mary Walton (1991) reports that midway through his first lecture, Deming "was overcome with a sense of déjà vu. He was not talking to the right people. Enthusiasm for statistical techniques would burn out in Japan as it had at home unless he could somehow reach the people in charge."

Deming received support from Ichiro Ishikawa, president of JUSE and head of the *Keidanren*, the powerful Japanese Federation of Eco-

---

[2]In his book *Managing Quality*, David A. Garvin (1988) of the Harvard Business School says that one of the CCS trainers, W.S. Magil, is sometimes "regarded as the father of statistical quality control in Japan. He first advocated its use in a lecture in 1945-46 and successfully applied its techniques to vacuum tube production at NEC in 1946."

nomic Organizations. Ishikawa wanted to impress upon Japanese industrial leaders the urgency of Japan's situation and the need for them to rethink their own management philosophies. Ishikawa invited twenty-one of the nation's top industrial executives to a dinner meeting with Deming. Many of them had been Ishikawa's students at the university, and still regarded him with the great reverence reserved for one's *sensei*, as is the deeply-rooted practice in Japan. Everyone showed up, and paid full attention to Deming, the tall, authoritative *gaijin*.[3]

At this first dinner with Japan's top industrial leaders, Deming drove home the point that, without the full support of top-level management, the quality revolution Japanese industry so desperately needed would be doomed from the start. It's not enough, Deming warned, to have a cadre of willing workers, all doing their best. The workers' efforts must be guided by the analysis of data and by what Deming would later call a system of profound knowledge, including a deep understanding of human psychology, learning theory, and variation within systems (Deming 1990). Deming told the Japanese to view their customers as the last and most important people on their production lines—a new idea for Japanese industrialists. He told them that quality is that which satisfies, even delights, the customer, and they must, therefore, go to their customers and ask them what they want. He suggested that they conduct door-to-door surveys and invest company resources in market research.

Deming emphasized the importance of eliminating production errors before they occur because defects require reworking, or scrapping, and are costly and wasteful. End-of-line inspection is also costly and wasteful because the inspector adds no value to the goods produced. In fact, Deming told his Japanese audiences that the inspector's presence often suggests to the line workers that their mistakes will be caught down the line so they needn't pay close attention to the quality of their work. This, he argued, is a costly and self-defeating attitude.

At the end of his speech, Deming pledged to the assembled industrial leaders that, if they followed his advice and made quality their number one priority, consumers worldwide would be clamoring for Japanese products within five years. Even Deming himself privately

---

[3]According to accepted Japanese tradition, a student's inferior position to his or her *sensei*, or teacher, does not change with the student's advancing age or accomplishments. It is expected that teachers will call students by their school names throughout life. Thus, the teacher's status permits him to call even the prime minister by an informal variation of his given name, while the prime minister must refer always to his teacher in the formal reverential term: *Sensei. Gaijin* is the Japanese word for "foreigner."

thought his estimate optimistic. And yet, amazingly, it took only four years for his prophesy to begin to be realized.

In 1954, JUSE extended an invitation to lecture to a second noted American statistical expert, Joseph M. Juran. Juran's seminars reinforced Deming's earlier teaching. Juran told the Japanese that management, not the production worker, is most accountable for the organization's performance. In *Juran on Planning for Quality*, Juran (1988) stresses the need for management to carefully plan quality into the production process, to monitor the quality of products throughout the production process, and to improve quality at a rapid rate. Juran writes that good planning requires that a dependable process be developed. If the process is not dependable, goals will not be consistently achieved.

Juran (1988) defines quality as "fitness for use" and "freedom from defects." He, like Deming, emphasizes the need to be attentive to the customers' perceptions of quality. The idea that the quest for quality must be an ongoing, never-ending process, is expressed graphically in Juran's "Spiral of Progress in Quality" with its cycle: Customers-Product Development-Operations-Marketing-Customers. The quality process begins and ends with the customer.

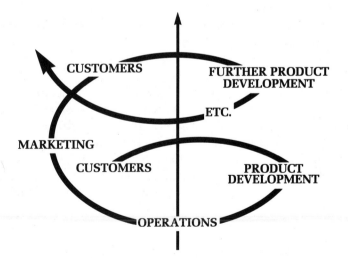

Juran told the Japanese to think of customers as "all persons who are impacted by our processes and our products," not just clients. He taught that there are internal as well as external customers. Juran (1988, p. 8) defines internal customers as "persons or organizations who are part of our company." External customers are "persons who are not part of our company but who are impacted by our products."

Juran (1988, p. 10) stresses the two-way relationship between customers and suppliers. "Customers provide their suppliers with requisitions, specifications, feedback on product performance, and so on. The customer becomes a supplier and the supplier becomes a customer."

About the time Juran was first visiting Japan, the Japanese were discovering the writings of another American quality expert, Armand Feigenbaum, who had served as the head of quality for General Electric. Feigenbaum was in contact with Hitachi, Toshiba, and other Japanese companies. Those companies spread his ideas of "Total Quality Control," which "required the involvement of all functions in the quality process, and not simply manufacturing. Otherwise, quality would be inspected and controlled after the fact and not built in at an early stage" (Garvin 1988, p.183).

Deming, Juran, and Feigenbaum each spoke of the need for organizations to make quality their first priority. Their teachings were based on the idea that production goals cannot be consistently achieved unless attention is paid to the processes leading to those goals. Processes must be continually improved so that products can be continually improved.

The Japanese took to heart the lessons Deming, Juran, Feigenbaum, and their CCS colleagues from Bell Labs and Western Electric shared with them in the late 1940s and early 1950s. As a result, "quality" is now the byword of Japanese industry. To honor and celebrate the quality achievements of Japanese and foreign companies, JUSE established the Deming Prize, named in honor of their American *sensei*. The award is given annually to those companies demonstrating the greatest improvements in the quality of their processes and products.[4]

---

[4]The American equivalent is the Malcolm Baldridge Award, established by an act of the United States Congress in 1987. JUSE asked Juran for permission to name an award after him, to be presented to the best of the Deming Prize recipients, but Juran declined, perhaps because he credits the Japanese themselves with the transformation they have achieved. Juran has said (Garvin 1988, p. 184): "I did indeed lecture in Japan as reported, and I did bring something new to them—a structured approach to quality. I also did the same thing for a great many other countries, yet none of these attained the results achieved by the Japanese. So who performed the miracle?"

# Total Quality Revisited in the United States

While the work of Deming, Juran, Feigenbaum, and other Americans was contributing to the economic miracle of postwar Japan, American industry and American society in general was happily—perhaps arrogantly—basking in the warm, reassuring glow of economic and military superpowerdom. Cars and other products were made not to last, but to self-destruct. "Planned obsolescence" became an accepted fact of life. Taylorism thrived. "How little quality can we get away with?" too often reflected the philosophy of American industry and commerce.

Disturbed by this attitude, Philip Crosby, an industrial consultant at ITT, joined his elder quality experts in preaching the gospel of "quality first" to American companies. He reinforced the idea that quality doesn't increase the cost of production, but lowers it. In *Quality Is Free*, Crosby 1980) argues that the putting the best possible resources in at the front end of a process will more than pay for the investment later. Mistakes in business are costly, in terms of lost time, lost profits, lost customers, and lost opportunities for growth and learning. Compared with such costs, doing the right thing the first time around is considerably less expensive.

Finally, in the late 1970s American industry started taking note of Japanese successes in the international marketplace. The U.S. trade deficit was growing larger every year, as goods produced in this country were shunted aside even by domestic consumers in favor of goods made in more quality-conscious societies, including Japan, Korea, and Germany. Some U.S. executives went to Japan to nose around, trying to uncover the "secret" of Japanese success. There they saw groups of workers huddled around in what seemed to be small discussion groups. These groups were the result of a nationwide "Quality Circle" movement that began to sweep Japan in the early 1960s. Quality Circles (QCs) are groups of workers who meet at their workplace to explore ways to improve their work and their work environment. QC members' efforts focus on their own self-development as well as development of others. A primary goal is to get all of their fellow workers involved in the improvement process. The American executives who saw these QC's were determined to use them back in the United States.

Unfortunately, QC's didn't work in American business, where they were imposed upon workers from above. QC's in American factories and organizations soon turned into gripe sessions, and eventually were abandoned. The executives who brought the QC concept from Japan neglected to understand the larger Japanese culture of which QC's were only a small part. In Japan, all workers are honored. The company president has honor, the garbage collector has honor, the smallest merchant has honor. Japan is certainly a highly stratified and status-conscious society, but the willingness of workers to labor with great self-discipline for a common corporate cause is culturally ingrained in the Japanese work ethic. To not give one's best is dishonorable and disgraceful. To not give honor to others is also disgraceful. Japanese Quality Circles operate within such an ethos; American QC's generally did not. Also, Japanese workers were empowered to make changes in their work processes based upon discoveries made in their Quality Circles; American workers were, in some cases, only permitted to offer suggestions to management, which largely ignored their ideas.

Kaoru Ishikawa, Ichiro Ishikawa's son and a noted quality expert in his own right, writes in *What Is Total Quality Control? The Japanese Way* that a number of differences exist between the Japanese and the Americans in their approaches to quality work. For example, in Japan, quality is every worker's business; in the United States, quality is often delegated to a division so that the idea of quality becomes compartmentalized within the organization. Some people are in charge of quality, most are not. Kaoru Ishikawa (1985, p. 25) says of Taylorism: "If people are treated like machines, work becomes uninteresting and unsatisfying. Under such conditions, it is not possible to expect products with good quality and high reliability. The rate of absenteeism and the rate of turnover are the measures one can use in determining the strengths and weaknesses of management style and worker morale in any company."

Ishikawa echoes the findings of recent surveys done in the United States when he suggests that the secret of success in business and in life is not found solely in the amount of money one earns, but also (and more importantly) in the satisfaction of doing one's work well, in the "happiness coming from cooperating with others and from being recognized by others," and in the joy of personal growth, which, he says, includes the following:

- experiencing the satisfaction that comes from being able to utilize one's own abilities to the fullest and from growing as a person;
- having self-confidence, and becoming a self-fulfilled person; and
- using one's own brain, working voluntarily, and in this way contributing to society (Ishikawa 1985, pp. 27-8).

Kaoru Ishikawa goes on to point out that the work group in Japan is like a family. Employees are hired for a lifetime, and this practice, according to Ishikawa (1985), "can be a desirable system from the points of view of humanity, democracy, and management."[5] Such ideas have too infrequently found fertile soil in modern American culture which is predicated upon tight top-down control, the arrogance of unlimited disparity in the compensation of employees and bosses, and a mindless preoccupation with bottom-line results even at the risk of organizational suicide. The data were there for all to see. American productivity and the nation's economic health were clearly declining; marriages, corporate profits, and general civility were all heading south, and people just didn't seem to care about quality anymore. Something was going very wrong, and everyone wondered what it could be.

A part of the answer came in 1980, with the broadcast of an NBC-TV documentary entitled "If Japan Can, Why Can't We?" The program focused on the work Deming had done in Japan, and the ways his teachings had helped the postwar Japanese economy to rebuild with dedication to quality and continuous improvement. The morning after the broadcast, Deming's phone began to ring off the hook as Ford, General Motors, and a host of other American companies sought his help, immediately if not sooner.

Deming's teachings, and that of other Quality consultants in business and education, continue to point our society, our businesses, and our educational systems in new and promising directions. Today, Schools of Quality—those schools that have dedicated themselves to continuous improvement for all of their people—are beginning to study and implement the philosophy of Total Quality, as expressed by Deming in his Fourteen Points (Deming 1986) and in what I have called the Four Pillars of Schools of Quality (See Chapter 4).

Deming encourages educators to create school environments in which strong relationships of mutual respect and trust replace fear, suspicion, and division; and in which leadership from administrators and policymakers empowers students and teachers (as front-line workers of the school) to make continuous improvements in the work they do together. The development of everyone's "yearning for learning" is all-important in Schools of Quality; grades and other symbols of learning are far less significant. Deming, in fact, opposes the use of grades altogether: "Abolish grades (A, B, C, D) in school, from toddlers up through the university. When graded, pupils put emphasis on the grade, not on learning" (Deming 1992).

---

[5]This practice is beginning to change in Japan as major corporations lay off workers during hard economic times.

The school, says Deming, should be a place where students, teachers, administrators, and others are able to take pride and joy in their work. It is the responsibility of administrators—the top management of schools —to remove the barriers that prevent this from being the daily experience of students and teachers.

Mass inspection in the factory is inherently wasteful, Deming states. Whenever inspection is relegated to the end of the production line, substandard products must be removed from the end of the assembly line, then sent back to the beginning for retooling or thrown on the trash heap. This, he observes, is possible (and wasteful) in the factory. But it is not possible to apply this solution to the young people who come through their educational process, failing at the end to achieve their potentials or, in some cases, even the minimum standards set by the school for graduation. Assessment should not wait until the end of the educational process, whether that process is a unit, a course, or the 13 years of schooling between kindergarten and the end of the senior year. Assessment for diagnostic and prescriptive purposes should inform every point along the line in the educational production process, providing teachers and students with a solid foundation for continuous improvement toward optimal success, rather than a judgemental "mark" or other end-of-the-line symbols of learning.

All of this cannot be done, Deming insists, without the strongest possible leadership from the top of the organization. A "constancy of purpose for improvement," supported by vigorous programs of training and retraining, will enable school leaders to take decisive action to accomplish the transformation over time (See Appendix 3).

The message is clear. But is anyone really listening? What is blocking our path, and how can we identify and remove these obstacles? What keeps us from becoming better and better, continually fulfilling and expanding our potentials, growing in joy and wisdom every day?

The answers may not be readily apparent until we look carefully at the cultural paradigm into which we were born, raised, and now live. We are a part of our society's cultural paradigm, just as a fish is part of its watery environment. And yet, our cultural paradigm—our deeply ingrained societal and personal predispositions of thought, emotions, and behavior—are largely invisible to us. "Water? What water?" the fish might say if it could communicate with us. "I don't know anything about the water you speak of. All I know is that this is my home, and this is the way I live."

# 3

## Learning a New Way to Swim

When my new friends Susan and Ted invited me and a few others to their home for an evening of slides taken on a trip to Europe, I was excited. I had travelled through some of the places on their itinerary so I was eager to discover their perspectives on the people they had met, the ways the people live, and the ideas they shared with Susan and Ted.

"Okay, now here's the first picture. Here we are at the airport, waving goodbye," Susan began.

"Our flight was two hours late," Ted added. We all commiserated. Airport delays: The scourge of modern travel.

"Okay, here we are in Europe. I think that's Big Ben behind us there. It's hard to tell. It was cloudy that day," Ted explained.

"Next picture!" Susan announced. "Oops! Ted, we should have taken this one out. Sorry, everybody. That's a blurry one." Ted scooped the slide from the tray.

"Okay, here I am in front of a church," Susan continued. "Where was this, honey?"

"Rome, I think," Ted replied. "The scenery was just spectacular!" We all agreed: Spectacular scenery.

This whirlwind tour went on for a while. Finally I asked, "What were the people like?"

"You mean the people on the tour?" Susan asked. "Oh, they were all very nice, very friendly folks."

"No," I replied. "I mean, what were the people like who live there? What kind of work do they do? What do they do in their spare time?"

Ted seemed mildly irritated by my questions, "We didn't have much time for that," he responded. "You know how tours can be—on the bus, off the bus, on the bus."

Susan shrugged and said, "Anyway, we *did* seven countries in ten days!"

It was as if Ted and Susan could now check off seven more countries on their list of experiences acquired. Great Britain? Check! France? Check! Luxembourg? Nope, next time! Metaphorically, I thought, they had just collected seven nations, and put them into their pockets for safekeeping. The slides served as proof of ownership.

I suspect that, for Susan and Ted, life's meaning has much to do with acquiring and possessing. The prominent psychologist Erich Fromm referred to this way of thinking and behaving as the "having mode" of living.

"The having mode of existence is not established by an alive, productive process between subject and object; it makes *things* of both object and subject. The relationship is one of deadness, not aliveness" (Fromm 1976). Thus, a rich opportunity for growth and learning and the expansion of one's universe may rationally be sacrificed for the things acquired, or for symbols of those things. It's impossible to actually carry the continent back home so symbolic slides must suffice. Fromm distinguishes this "having mode" from another way of living, which he calls the "being mode of existence."

Western culture, is increasingly focused on *having*, not on *being* (and certainly not on *becoming*). This is the "water" in which we American fish swim, most often without knowing its depth and breadth, or the pressures it puts on us from all sides. The having mode is at the core of our daily lives, and informs—often misinforms—our perceptions, thoughts, feelings, and behavior. This having mode lies at the heart of what remains of our production-oriented work ethic. It influences the ways we perceive and treat ourselves, how we love ourselves and others, the ways we learn and remember, and our ways of knowing and understanding. The having mode is well-known to students and teachers.

Fromm points out that

> students in the having mode aim to hold onto what they "learned," either by entrusting it firmly to their memories or by carefully guarding their notes. They do not have to produce or create anything new. In fact, having-type individuals feel rather

disturbed by new thoughts or ideas about a subject, because the new puts into question the information they already have. Indeed, to one for whom having is the main form of relatedness to the world, ideas that cannot be pinned down (or penned down) are frightening—like everything else that grows and changes and, therefore, is not controllable" (Fromm 1976).

The having mode, expressed by scores of Western writers, thinkers, and artists, is grounded in the notion that living things are essentially unconnected unless their relationship is competitive, adversarial, and mutually exclusive. This perspective goes back as far as Aristotle, who divided all of human sensation into sight, taste, smell, touch, and hearing. Yet, today, we know that humans have more than thirty bodily sensory functions, virtually all of which are interconnected (Leonard 1978).

Aristotle and other great thinkers of ancient Greece perceived their world in logical dichotomies: good and bad, right and wrong, male and female, winners and losers. In this view of nature, polar opposites are perpetually at war with each other for ultimate control. Their mutual exclusivity makes life a contest in which only the stronger element of each dichotomy survive.

| US | THEM |
|---|---|
| RIGHT ANSWER | WRONG ANSWERS |
| LIFE | DEATH |
| MALE | FEMALE |
| WINNER | LOSERS |
| WHITE | BLACK |
| BODY | MIND |
| INTELLECT | EMOTION |
| PAIN | PLEASURE |

## Dichotomies

Students in the being mode, according to Fromm, develop a wider perspective than their having-mode peers:

Instead of being passive receptacles of words and ideas, they listen, they hear, and most important, they receive and they respond in an active, productive way. What they listen to stimulates their own thinking processes. New questions, new ideas, new perspectives arise in their minds. Their listening is an alive process . . . . They do not simply acquire knowledge that they can take home and memorize. Each student has been affected and has changed: each is different after [the lesson] than he or she was before it (Fromm 1976).

This view of the world springs from the ancient Confucian tradition, graphically represented by the yin-yang, an ancient oriental symbol of wholeness:

Like the polar opposite dichotomies, the yin-yang is divided into two parts. In the yin-yang, however, each half depends upon the other half for its existence. Neither has meaning without the other. Nothing can exist without its opposite. To know Good is impossible without knowing Evil. To know what is Wrong, one must also know what is Right. Each element is balanced by its opposite. Life consists not of adversarial dichotomies, but of *dualities*—polar opposites that add richness and meaning to one another.

Notice that within the light half of the yin-yang there is a dark dot, and within the dark half there is a light dot of the same size. This signifies that everything contains a small element of its opposite. In the evil that befalls each of us there are the seeds of good. From death springs life, from endings come beginnings. Thus, life is viewed as a cycle or spiral, a continuous wheel of existence known to the people of India as the Great Mandala. Life in the Eastern tradition is of one cloth, neverending and interconnected.

In this worldview, the integrity of the product—especially in the long term—is always dependent upon the integrity of the process used in getting the product.

The following is a diagram of a single process. The beginning of the process is Point A. The goal, or product, is Point B. The line between the two points represents a series of moments during the process.

A– – – – – – – – – – –→ B

Point A (the beginning of the process) and Point B (the realization of the product, or goal, or result) are actually points in time. There are other points in time to the left of A, to the right of B, and between A and B. All of those points are also part of a larger, ongoing process, of which this A-B segment is only a small part.

– – – – – –→A– – – – – – – – – – –→B – – – – – –→

Product-oriented people focus only on the results at the end of the process (point B). They are comfortable in dichotomistic modes of thinking and acting, so they tend to view the end product as an objective separate from the entire process. If they concern themselves at all with the process leading to the objective, it is only to think of it as a nuisance, not as an opportunity for growth and learning. All effort is thus expended on the speedy acquisition of the goal. The product is viewed as a static end-point. Once the objective is "captured," it is held inviolable, protected against mutation and encroachment, and thus, kept from improvement. The value of the process is found solely in the results: The proof is in the pudding.

A– – – – – – – – – – –→B

By viewing the product as a fixed end-point, product-oriented people figuratively capture the product and store it away in a box for safe keeping. The box I've drawn around Point B shows that the outcome is enclosed in this way, protected for all time. Ted and Susan put their "seven countries" into this sort of box. We educators have traditionally put students' test scores into a kind of box, too. The problem is, while students' grades stay permanently inscribed in the appointed boxes in teachers' gradebooks, the learning processes and products symbolized by those grades are constantly being transmuted: Some elements of the learning processes become incorporated into the students' ways of dealing with real life, while other "learnings" have a post-exam halflife of, perhaps, three minutes. Also, the grades in those gradebooks don't show how much the teachers—or their school as a "learning organization"—has learned through the process.

The person who is process-oriented understands the importance of setting worthy goals, but also knows that the process is what makes goals achievable. Process-oriented people, therefore, take great pains to plan the process carefully, and monitor and adapt the process constantly to ensure continuous improvement. They know that the quality of their input into the process will in large part determine the quality of the product, or output.

They view the product not as a static end-point, but as a dynamic access-point, leading to other processes and products.

Process-oriented people assess the quality of the processes as well as the products that flow from those processes.

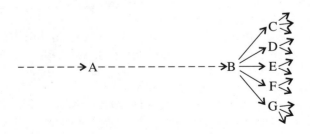

This view reflects the fact that every process takes place within a network of other processes. This network is called a *system*. Elements of a system are interconnected, so each process affects other processes within the system. When all processes are of the highest possible quality, working synergistically (like the students in Bob's class or the players on his football team when "everything is clicking"), we can say that the system is *optimized*. Whenever any process within a system is functioning below its peak-performance level, or when elements of the system are working at cross-purposes or with only the product in mind, the entire system (including its processes) is *suboptimized*.

When a system is suboptimizing, it is most helpful to assess the entire system, including all of its processes. Shewhart identified two causes of system suboptimization: *random variation* and *assignable causes*, later designated by Deming as *common causes* of variation and *special causes* of variation. A common cause of variation is one that relates to the functioning of the system as a whole; a special cause of variation occurs when a process is failing within the system. Deming and others suggest that, in any system, 85 percent or more of the reasons for suboptimization can be traced to the way the system is set up (failure due to common causes). Less than 15 percent of the failures are due to individual processes or people malfunctioning within a fully functioning system (failure due to special causes).

The implications for education are significant. The classroom teacher and his students are part of a learning system within the confines of the room, and they are part of a much larger system within the school building, which, in turn, is part of the school district, families and community, the state, the nation, and the world. The optimization of any one of these systems is dependent to some extent upon the functioning of the others because the processes of every system affect the entire system, positively or negatively. Every experience, inside and outside of the classroom, affects the learning that can take place in the classroom. According to Chester Finn, between birth and graduation from high school, a person spends only 9 percent of his or her life in school. Ninety-one percent of the young person's life is lived *outside* the school building. It is obvious that processes and systems outside the classroom affect the processes and systems within it.

What inputs are part of the process of growing up for today's young person? And what are the products of those processes? What impacts are made on youngsters by television, advertisements, movies, the neighborhood, the kinds of food they eat, their family structures, and loving parental discipline or its absence? What about our culture's growing commercialization? The growing alienation of people from one another? The mounting pressures of time and money? What effects do these factors—all inputs from society into the systems of education—have on educators and students?

How do business successes and failures influence educators' ability to do their best possible work? Do educators and business people see each other as possible partners, or do they view one another in more dichotomistic terms? Do parents and teachers view one another as partners in the continuous improvement of children's lives? Do parents accept their rightful role as the primary teachers of their children, and are teachers supportive of that role for parents?

How do state and federal regulations affect the work that administrators do, and how does all of this provide inputs into the micro-learning system of the classroom teacher and her students?

Educators must consider the ramifications of these and other issues. When we neglect to factor these inputs into our equations in school restructuring, strategic planning, curriculum design, teacher training, and the other work of our profession, we very surely design suboptimization and failure into our systems.

Total Quality Management provides educators with a conceptual framework for addressing these issues in our schools. TQM gives us a philosophy and a set of tools to understand—through data analysis—what our systems are made of, what they are capable of doing, and the reasons and ways suboptimization is taking place. Unfortunately, most organizations—including businesses and schools all around the world—still function in a Tayloresque manner with hierarchical, top-down authoritarian power structures based upon compliance, control, and command; little true empowerment of front-line workers to create, monitor, and control their own work processes; little real participation by workers in the governance of the organization; and more attention paid to end products than to the processes essential to increased productivity.

In this virtual prescription for suboptimization, the efforts of an organization are not focused on educating the customer about quality or delighting the customer, or even serving the customer. Suppliers are left to their own devices, and often viewed as threats, or as inconsequential to the work of the organization. People within the organization do not treat one another as essential suppliers and customers, so the synergy that might "make things click" never even begins.

An organization with such a dichotomistic product-orientation makes it difficult for people associated with the organization to learn from each other. What should be a growing, continuously improving, optimizing, learning organization is instead a place where people communicate less and less with each other while they grow more and more disaffected from one another, from their bosses, and from their work. This is particularly ironic and tragic when the erstwhile "learning organization" is a school, where the optimization of the system is so crucial for our collective future, as well as for the personal futures of our children.

Peter Senge (1990) points out in *The Fifth Discipline: The Art and Practice of the Learning Organization* that "as the world becomes more complex and dynamic, work must become more 'learningful.' It's no longer sufficient to have one person learning for the organization, 'figuring it out' from the top, with everyone else following the orders of the 'grand strategist.' To truly excel in the future, organizations will have to tap the commitment and capacity to learn of people at *all* levels in an organization." A learning organization, says Senge (1990), is "continually expanding its capacity to create its future." In the language of Total Quality Management, a true learning organization optimizes its entire system—including processes and products—by empowering everyone, especially front-line workers—students and teachers in the case of schools—to continuously improve their work.

Teachers and students, as the schools' front-line workers, must be empowered to put forth their best efforts and understand the processes, systems, and opportunities for continual growth and improvement. In fact, an essential aspect of learning how to improve thinking and learning capabilities is learning how to expand our perceptual awareness. Empathy and the development of a wider perceptual field are linked. People who are aware of their own thoughts, feelings, and behaviors are often best able to understand the thoughts, feelings, and behaviors of others. Greater awareness of the whole, of the system of processes (of which the individual is a part), is a natural extension of the quest for continuous improvement, which is at the heart of Total Quality. In a chapter entitled "Toward Process-Oriented Persons," the University of Maryland's Louise Berman (1968) writes: "Highly process-oriented persons do not stagnate under the debris of nonessential or nonmeaningful aspects of life. They see purposes to the degree of change and movement they plan for themselves." They are in the process of self-actualization, otherwise known as continuous improvement.

It baffles me that the process of learning in today's classrooms so infrequently includes reflection by teachers and students on the optimization of the learning they do together. The routine is always the same: Begin the unit, teach the unit, give the students a test, correct the test, return the test, review the 'right' answers with the class, collect the tests, and record the grades. Then move on the next unit. If we continue this practice, how will students learn to use experiences from past units to improve the work they do on future units?

To help students engage in constant improvement, we must make the teacher-student learning system the focal point of instruction so that the ways teachers and students interact in the learning process can be continually fine-tuned.

Educators who focus on this teacher-student interaction and understand and apply this process/systems philosophy know that it requires a lifestyle change. It takes a dedication to the process of continuous improvement, for oneself and for others in the "system"—whether that system is a group of friends, a workplace, a family, or any other set of interconnections in life. When you apply this philosophy of Total Quality to yourself and your relations with other people, places, and things, you take on a kind of interpersonal, planetary stewardship. For many of us "American fish," this philosophy provides a new and challenging way to swim in the waters of our families, our workplaces, and our communities.

# 4

## Reconsidering the Better Mousetrap

"**B**uild a better mousetrap, and the world will beat a path to your door!" Remember that old adage?

Mousetraps are good to have around. *If* you have mice.

The key idea, however, is not to invent a better way to kill mice effectively, but to discover a way to not have mice around in the first place. In TQM parlance this means it's better to create high-quality processes so your system operates optimally, than to put up with unwanted products you will need to "inspect out" at the end of the production line. If you can fix the system so that those pesky mice don't find their way to your domicile, you won't need a better mousetrap. In fact, you won't need any kind of mousetrap.

Total Quality Management is not a program for building a better mousetrap in a business, school, or community organization. In fact, TQM is not really a program at all. It isn't a panacea for curing all the ills of your organization's staff, or those of the community or anyone or anything else. And it most certainly isn't a "flavor of the month" reform effort. It is not something you will "do" this month or this year, as Susan and Ted "did" their seven countries in ten days and then put their experiences and their symbolic slides aside.

TQM is, as we have seen, a new way of thinking and living that pervades all aspects of life. When the TQM philosophy is fully implemented in an organization, it becomes the heart and soul of the organization's way of operating. It becomes the new "water" in which the organization's fish swim. It must be accepted as "the way things are done around here" by everyone in the organization, and by everyone who influences and is influenced by the organization's system. TQM requires consistent effort by the entire team, working together toward common objectives based upon an accepted vision and mission, and using quantitative and qualitative data to measure how well the system is meeting the needs of all stakeholders inside and outside of the organization. How long must this commitment to Total Quality go on? As W. Edwards Deming has said: "Forever!" (Gottlieb 1984). What we're really talking about, of course, is nothing less than a paradigm shift. In *Future Edge*, Joel Barker (1992, p. 31) quotes Adam Smith's definition of a paradigm as "a shared set of assumptions. The paradigm is the way we perceive the world; water to the fish. The paradigm explains the world to us and helps us to predict its behavior."

In *The Aquarian Conspiracy*, Marilyn Ferguson (1980, p. 228) describes a new paradigm of education, which "looks to the nature of learning rather than methods of instruction. Learning, after all . . . is the process by which we have moved every step of the way since we first breathed; the transformation that occurs in the brain whenever new information is integrated, whenever a new skill is mastered. Learning is kindled in the mind of the individual. Anything else is mere schooling."

Schooling has tended to mirror business in its adherence to Taylor-esque qualities. Arthur C. Clarke (1986, p. 76) points out in *July 20, 2019: Life in the 21st Century* that there will need to be a paradigm shift in education's basic emphasis: "Our current educational system evolved to produce workers for the Industrial Revolution's factory-based economy, for work that requires patience, docility, and the ability to endure boredom. Students learned to sit in orderly rows, to absorb facts by rote, and to move as a group through the material regardless of individual differences in learning speed."

"But," Clarke points out, "no factory jobs will be left in 2019. Except for a few technicians to watch over control panels, tomorrow's factories will be automatic, with computers directing robot workers."

Barnard College President Ellen Futter (cited in Clarke 1986, p. 76) suggests: "We must give [students] certain key intellectual skills—analytical thinking, critical thinking, the ability to make judgements, to reason quantitatively, to balance opposed points of view. We must focus more on how to learn, how to think."

In such a learning environment, the school relinquishes its past role as a delivery system for discreet and often fragmented bits of data in the guise of curriculums. The school becomes, instead, a place where people (of all ages) cultivate their innate "yearning for learning," as Deming would say. Nothing is more important than keeping that yearning alive. Nothing is more important than cultivating a love of learning, of personal growth, and of getting better and better while helping others to do the same.

In the new paradigm of learning, schools learn how to create processes that encourage the continuous improvement of one's abilities, the expansion of one's interests, and the growth of one's character. Such an education is good for the individual student, good for the economy, and good for the commonweal we call society (Bonstingl 1992, p. 67).However, according to management consultant Robert F. Lynch (1991, p. 64), today "our entire educational system is designed to teach people to do things the one right way as defined by the authority figure. We are taught to recite what we hear or read without critically interacting with the information as it moves in and out of short-term memory. In this exchange, the information leaves no tracks, and independent thinking skills are not developed."

In *A Whack on the Side of the Head: How To Unlock Your Mind for Innovation*, Roger von Oech (1983, p. 21) asks, "Where do you learn how to think? One important source is your formal schooling . . . . Your educational training gives you many of the concepts you use to order and understand the world." Thus, the paradigm of the school becomes for many the paradigm of life.

Von Oech continues:

> Much of our educational system, however, is geared toward teaching people the one right answer. By the time the average person finishes college, he or she will have taken over 2,600 tests, quizzes, and exams . . . . Thus, the right answer approach becomes deeply ingrained in our thinking. This may be fine for some mathematical problems where there is in fact only one right answer. The difficulty is that most of life doesn't present itself in this way. Life is ambiguous; there are many right answers—all depending on what you are looking for. But if you think there is only one right answer, then you will stop looking as soon as you find one.

> Looking to the authority figure for the one right answer can be deadly

in the business world, where a variety of competing "right answers" vie for implementation and adoption by producers and consumers alike. In my article (Bonstingl 1992), "The Total Quality Classroom," I tell the story of a new employee, a college student whom my friend Jim had hired to work at his family-owned Italian restaurant. One day, this new employee, Lisa, stunned Jim with the question: "How many mushrooms should I put on a 12-inch pizza?"

Jim thought it was a strange question, but Lisa explained that at her previous job as a pizzamaker for one of the big chain restaurants she and her fellow employees had to follow a thick rulebook. And the rulebook specified the exact number of mushroom slices for every size pizza.

"She wanted the right answer," Jim told me. "She wanted *my* right answer, not the customer's right answer."

It's an easy step from seeking teachers' and professors' right answers to seeking employers' right answers. How many of our students come through their schooling believing that the end-user of their work is the teacher? How many young people realize that their education is *their* education, a tool for what should be their own self-improvement? "How many mushrooms on a 12-inch pizza?" Frederick Winslow Taylor would have been delighted!

Jim thought for a moment, then replied with his own question (Socrates would have been delighted!): "Do *you* like pizza?"

"Sure, I like pizza," Lisa responded.

"Okay," Jim answered, "how many mushrooms do *you* like on *your* pizzas? Just do for your customers what you would like if you were them. You decide!"

Jim's central tenet, one shared with every employee in the restaurant's thorough an ongoing training process, is simple: Always keep the customer in mind. Customers have, as Lisa would soon find out, a wide variety of preferences. There were lots of "right answers" for her to find out from them. Lots of different, and often *differing*, perspectives to consider.

In the world of the future, with increasing diversity and global interconnections, our young people will need to be as comfortable with answers from people who live halfway around the world as they are with the opinions of their friends and neighbors. The "one right answer" just isn't right anymore. Dichotomistic, product-oriented modes of thought and behavior do not fit the needs of the global village, which must be viewed as one unified system of diverse people and processes.

Today, in Schools of Quality, a new process-oriented paradigm of continuous learning and improvement is beginning to replace the old Tayloresque, product-oriented, fear-driven paradigm of teaching and testing (See Appendix 4). School leaders with whom I have worked to create Schools of Quality agree that there are four essential elements of this new Total Quality educational paradigm. I call these four characteristics the Four Pillars of Schools of Quality:

1. A primary focus on suppliers and customers.
2. Constant dedication to continuous improvement.
3. A systems/process orientation.
4. Strong and consistent Total Quality leadership from top management.

Each of these Four Pillars has many implications for the work of schools and school leaders.

# A Primary Focus on Suppliers and Customers

As with other fiscally based enterprises, schools are in business to satisfy their customers and to maximize opportunities to serve and delight them. Every thriving business must satisfy the needs not only of *external* customers (those who buy and use the organization's product or service), but also of *internal* customers (people within the organization who help to create the service or product and those who are affected by their work). Within an organization, all workers must collaborate with their suppliers—the people who provide the materials used in the production process—to make sure the suppliers' work meets the internal customer's specific needs. Everyone inside every organization is a supplier as well as a customer, and therefore chains and networks of partnership and mutual support (externally as well as internally) must be built to optimize the effectiveness of the organizational system.

In Schools of Quality, and also in their communities, everyone is both a customer and a supplier. A clear, personalized understanding of these roles is essential for optimal systematic improvement to take place.

Our schools' customers are, primarily, our students and their families. They are, or should be, the main beneficiaries of our schools' work. As trustees of young students, parents are initially *primary* customers of their children's school, but as children grow and mature, parents necessarily make the transition to *secondary* customers of the school, enabling their children as *primary* customers of the school to take control of their own educational journeys.

Parents and families, as suppliers to the school, entrust their tax monies and their children to the school's care. Parents are also, in a certain sense, suppliers who must provide their children with their very first lessons in responsibility, understanding, and compassion, as well as the pre- and post-natal psychological and physiological nutrition required for mental and physical health. It is the responsibility of Schools of Quality and their communities to work with these parent-family suppliers to optimize children's potentials to benefit from the learning processes provided at school.

Students, working alongside their teachers, are not only the primary customers of the school, but also the schools' frontline workers. Students, as workers, produce their own continuous improvement of abilities, interests, and character. Their main focus must be the constant, authentic, and long-term improvement of self and others, rather than the acquisition of grades and other symbols of short-lived learning.

Teacher-student teams are the customers of the school administrators, who are the suppliers of a learning environment and educational context in which human potential is maximized and barriers to students' and teachers' pride and joy in working together are eliminated from the processes of the system.

Teachers are suppliers and customers of one another. The 5th grade teacher team finds out what the 6th grade teacher team expects of students. Effective, ongoing communication between building sites makes it possible for teachers at the elementary, middle, and high school levels to modify their work with students to better prepare them for the academic and social challenges they will encounter in future years.

The school board, setting the larger context for optimization of the school district as a working system, supplies policies that empower and enable their internal customers, the site and district administrators, to create a true learning organization in which micro-management is put aside in favor of genuine site-based management. As customers of the school board, administrators at every level must feel free to discuss their needs honestly and openly with the board, without reservation, intimidation, or fear. School boards and school administrators trained in TQM principles and practices view themselves as teammates with each other and with the teachers, students, staff, parents, families, businesses, and community members—all of whom are, or should be, partners in the progress of the schools' people and processes.

At the local, state, and federal levels, agencies whose policies influence school board and administration practices are suppliers of policy contexts to school boards and administrators. District school officials must help higher policymaking agencies view themselves as suppliers and teammates with school district and site administrators. Here again, the old Tayloresque model of compliance, control, and command gives way to a new model of teamwork and mutual dedication to continuous improvement of the entire system and its people and processes.

Secretarial staffs, bus drivers, groundskeepers, and other employees of the school district are also part of the overall system, and play active roles as suppliers and customers of each other and of teachers, students, administrators, and other stakeholders in Schools of Quality.

School leaders who spend time and other resources developing highly personalized customer/supplier relationships inside and outside of the school building reap abundant rewards in terms of the continuous improvement of the system and its processes. For example, administrators at Wilde Lake High School in Columbia, Maryland, are working closely with local businesspeople who employ Wilde Lake students after school hours. The employers join forces with the school to help their student employees improve their schoolwork. At the same time, the school gets valuable information from those businesses, in their role as current and prospective employers of Wilde Lake students, concerning the strengths and shortcomings of those young people's academic preparation for the world of work.

Other Schools of Quality determine what their customers and suppliers need by conducting focus groups with parents, students, administrators, teachers and other staff members, business people, and taxpayers who meet and critique the processes and products of the school system. Still others conduct surveys of staff, parents, community members, and students to find out how well the school and district are meeting the needs of all stakeholders. As Carl Marburger, who pioneered the creation of effective school-parent-community networking processes as co-founder of the National Committee for Citizens in Education, has said, schools and their stakeholders must move "beyond the bake sale" solutions to create positive, ongoing relationships of understanding and support *before* crises occur (Henderson et al. 1987). Focus groups, surveys, and other data-gathering and power-sharing instruments serve not only to inform school leaders and their staffs about the perceptions stakeholders have of the schools, but also to invite people to make personal contributions of time, ideas, energies, and even "yes" votes on essential bond issues—all of which help to make possible the school's continuous improvement process. Which brings us to the second of the Four Pillars of Quality Schools. . . .

# Constant Dedication to Continuous Improvement

In Total Quality organizations, including Schools of Quality, all individuals must be dedicated to self-improvement and the betterment—little by little, day by day—of other people in their spheres of influence. This, as we have seen, is what the Japanese call *kaizen*, a never-ending journey of improvement for oneself, one's family and friends, workmates, community, and, ultimately, the world. An idealistic and optimistic philosophy, to be sure, but one that actually works.

Rather than encouraging students to explore hidden talents and to build on previous successes and understandings, our tradition of schooling has all too often focused on students' failures, inadequacies, and limitations. The bell curve and other devices that create artificial scarcities of student success result in artificial limitations of individual and schoolwide success. Success in such a system is, by design, limited to a few "winners," while others are made to consider themselves and their work as mediocre or inferior.

While many traditional schools still view learning as a collection of linear, consecutive segments of one-way communication, Schools of Quality view the learning process as a spiral, with students' and teachers' energies directed toward unlimited continuous improvement, similar to Juran's Spiral of Progress in Quality, or a spiral-shaped PDSA Cycle, or a continuous Experience Pattern (perception—conceptualization—thought—action—reaction—perception, etc.) as shown in the diagram below (Bonstingl 1991).

Perception→Conceptualization→Thought→Action→Reaction

In this view of continuous learning, rather than serving as silent tabulae rasae or empty vessels to be filled by teachers, texts, and tests, students use their prior knowledge and understanding as the foundation for construction of new learning and the constant refinement of developing intelligences.

The spiral of learning is an old and familiar construct in the field of education. Hilda Taba (1971) introduced concept spirals in instructional practice a generation ago. Indeed, Socrates' approach might be viewed as essentially spiral, with the focus of questions leading students to ever-higher levels of understanding. Schools of Quality worldwide conceptualize optimal learning processes as spirals of continuous improvement. In the Alternative Secondary School for Economics, Hungary's first privately-funded, teacher-operated secondary school, the motto is "We are for the tadpoles." Growth is seen as a spiral, in which the school's "tadpoles" eventually develop into "frogs." The process of being a tadpole comes first, and has great internal integrity.

At the Centro de Educacion Natural e Integral (CENI) of Montevideo, Uruguay, students and teachers join together in a spiral journey of learning that takes them from the very concrete to the very abstract. "The children live and breathe the spirit of cooperation and sharing. . . . Good work is that which results in learning new information, is healthy for the body, and is shared by or offered to the group," according to Jeanette Stanko, who has done extensive on-site research into the operation of the school.

> In a learning environment where the children's prior knowledge
> is respected and valued and where they are allowed to
> manipulate, control, and question what they are learning about .
> . . . In this community, the teacher is more like a group guide or
> enabler, providing and setting up the learning experiences, but
> allowing the students to experiment, question, observe, and
> manipulate the environment at their own pace, in their own way
> (Stanko 1991).

In Schools of Quality, learning for everyone—students, teachers, administrators, and other staff—is viewed as a journey, not a series of destinations. Life itself is viewed as a journey with intrinsic merit if it is undertaken with a zest for living, a love of oneself and others, and a yearning for learning. Thus, the School of Quality is a true learning organization in which everyone is dedicated to continuous improvement of self, others, and the processes and systems of everyday life. In the classroom, teachers and students take time at the end of each unit to figure out how they did their work together, and how their collective and individual efforts might be fine-tuned in the following unit to maximize success and optimize collective and individual learning processes and systems.

Just as employees of many "learning" companies in Japan and the United States come together in Quality Circles on a regular basis to study ways of improving their individual and collective efforts, at some Schools of Quality, teachers, administrators, and other staff members are beginning to meet in QC's to discover ways of improving individually and collectively in their work with each other and with the students and other stakeholders. Teacher QC's most often meet on school time to discuss new ideas garnered from readings about their discipline and education in general. Often, QC's or their equivalent take the form of cross-disciplinary teacher discussions about methods, materials, and student progress. Such discussions often include benchmarking— monitoring of successful educational experiments from all around the world as possible models from which to learn and adopt new ideas for local educational environments and processes. Benchmarking is gaining favor in education, as well as in the world of business, because it encourages continuous improvement by everyone, allowing standards of performance to rise rapidly. In Napa, California, cross-disciplinary groups of teachers at Redwood Middle School have a common planning period each day while their students are taking physical education classes. Every tenth day, students are dismissed early, giving teacher teams the entire afternoon to plan and discuss ways of improving their individual and collective efforts toward continuous learning and improvement for themselves and their students. This common study and discussion time is what makes the school work—"the genius of the plan," according to Principal Harrell Miller, and is well worth the time invested.

This *kaizen* focus is also extended to faculty meetings at Redwood. There are two after-school faculty meetings each month, hosted on a revolving basis by an individual faculty member in a designated classroom area. During these meetings, the host teachers share new ideas about instructional methods, classroom environments, curriculums, and materials, and discuss issues of common concern. Faculty members walk away from these meetings energized and rededicated to the success of their common cause, the optimization of teacher and student successes.

Quality Circles work for students, too. At Glenwood Middle School in Maryland, small groups of students work in Support Teams known as "S-Teams" (a play on the word *esteem*). S-Team members pledge to support each others' efforts toward continuous academic and personal improvements. They become, in many cases, like families. Glenwood's S-Teams present their improvement efforts at schoolwide student government assemblies, patterned after the New England town meeting, where they dedicate themselves to school and community improvement projects as a natural extension of their own mutual support efforts (Bonstingl 1991).

At Carder Elementary School in Corning, New York, and at the Perry School in Erie, Pennsylvania, another kind of continuous improvement process is taking place. It is called the Koalaty Kid Project. A brainchild of Carder's spirited instructional staff, this project teaches students that "every kid is a Koalaty Kid" in a wide variety of ways. Pictures of the school's mascot, the koala, hang throughout the building. Stuffed koalas are available for snuggling during reading time, and a "real-life" koala (usually a parent in costume) is always present at the school's frequent assemblies to celebrate students' achievements and good efforts. "I caught you being good!" is a favorite slogan at Carder.

The Koalaty Kid program, which is now supported by Corning Incorporated and the American Society for Quality Control, has resulted in higher attendance, markedly increased student interest in reading, and an environment of empowerment for administrators, teachers, students, and the business and community people who are encouraged to drop by and read with students.

Koalaty Kid has grown by leaps and bounds, and now draws interest from educators around the world. David B. Luther, vice president of Corning and chair of the Koalaty Kid Steering Committee, wrote in the Koalaty Kid Manual (1991) that implementing this successful program

> requires thoughtful teamwork and rigorous and continuous reexamination. Koalaty Kid is based on the assumption that children want to learn and want to behave in acceptable ways, and will make a real effort to do so if the environment they're in promotes their self-esteem and stimulates their desire to achieve attainable goals. The dimension that Koalaty Kid brings to the picture is a systematic process for achieving the desired outcomes, and for continuous improvement. This process involves a team approach that includes not only teachers and administrators, but also students, parents, volunteers, and business partners.

Continuous improvement is an everyday part of life in Schools of Quality. During the more than two decades that Wilde Lake High School has operated, there has been no failure. Students keep improving their work during each quarter until the work merits at least a grade of C. According to Principal Bonnie Daniel, the school's insistence upon student mastery at a rigorous *minimum* C level has brought favorable attention from top colleges and universities to which Wilde Lake students apply for admission.

Daniel's own career mirrors the school's philosophy of continuous improvement. When the school began, she started as a secretary, becoming in turn an English teacher, department head, curriculum specialist, and district staff trainer, before returning to the school as principal. Total Quality depends upon this type of personal vision and effort, a constant journey of *kaizen* for self, family, friends, workmates, and the entire organization. If schools are to become our foremost "learning organizations," models for our other institutions to emulate, such dedication to *kaizen* must pervade all aspects of their processes and systems.

Which brings us to the third of the Four Pillars of Quality Schools . . .

# A Systems/Process Orientation

Quality products in schools, as in business, come from quality processes. In Schools of Quality, everyone understands that improvement of student outcomes can only be achieved, over the long run, when learning processes are being continuously improved by those on the front lines—teacher-student teams—and when the entire system supporting those processes is being continuously improved by administrators who create the context for optimal success within the school. Learning, by its very nature, transcends the school. Schools of Quality prepare young people for not only lifelong learning, but life-*wide* learning as well—learning that pervades every aspect of life's journey.[1]

All of the school's internal and external customers and suppliers, including all of its stakeholders, must be viewed as part of the school's operational system because each person's actions impact everyone else in the system. Total Quality Management tools and techniques, such as flowcharts and cause-effect diagrams, can be helpful in discovering who all of the "players" in the system really are, and what influences they have on the system. As members of the system begin to realize their essential interconnectedness, they can better understand what roles they play in fulfilling the potentials of the school and its people (see Appendix 1).

---

[1] I am indebted to Professor Jost Reischmann of the University of Tübingen, Germany, for sharing his concept of life-wide learning with me.

The most successful Schools of Quality build strong linkages with major stakeholders, recognizing them as essential contributors to schools' ongoing improvement processes. In Madison, Wisconsin, several neighboring school systems have joined forces with civic and business organizations and hospitals to form the Madison Area Quality Improvement Council (MAQIN), which works actively in various ways to support the schools' continuous improvement processes. In Erie, Pennsylvania, school leaders have combined efforts with government and business leaders to create a citywide Quality Council to improve all of Erie's products and services, including its educational products and services. This district's highly successful community effort to pull itself up by its own bootstraps has resulted in the establishment of the World Center for Community Excellence, located in downtown Erie, as an outreach organization to help other struggling communities in the process of continuous improvement through networking and community-building.

The same systems/process orientation necessary for Schools of Quality to establish networks of support in their quest for *kaizen* at a macro level is essential for learning and improvement to be optimized at the micro level, within each student. Research at the University of California over the past two decades shows that the deepest, most long-lasting learning takes place when it is *confluent* learning, merging the affective, cognitive, and psychomotor dimensions of learning. One of my first students described it this way: Pointing to his head and then his heart, he told me, "Mr. B., if you want to get me here, you gotta get me *here* first!" We now know that the three elements of the personal internal learning system are interlinked, and they work as processes within the larger human system. Yet, so much of our work with students, particularly at the upper grade levels and in postsecondary institutions, is focused on the cognitive realm. In Schools of Quality, caring environments are created by everyone, so that the heart can more easily join the head in the processes of *kaizen*.

Now let's look at our last Pillar of Quality:

# Strong and Consistent Total Quality Leadership from Top Management

For school leaders, this is the most important of the four essential characteristics of Schools of Quality. In the first of Deming's Fourteen

Points (see Appendix 3), he establishes the preeminent need for management to "create constancy of purpose for the improvement of product and service." Quality, insists Deming, cannot and must not be delegated. Responsibility for quality processes, systems, and outcomes rests with management. Workers, acting by themselves, cannot create the system-wide conditions under which quality processes take place. That is the job of management, which is entrusted with the responsibility of fully adopting this new Total Quality philosophy throughout the organization, building relationships of trust from the top down, empowering and enabling frontline workers to continuously improve by removing the barriers to their natural joy and pride of workmanship, and garnering the necessary resources to provide ongoing training in Total Quality principles and practices for management and workers. This applies to quality businesses, as well as Schools of Quality.

Most importantly, management must drive fear out of the organization. The old fear-based Taylor system of compliance, control, and command has no place in the modern workplace—business or school—where people must think creatively, work in self-directed teams, and build win-win cultures of mutual support for everyone's continuous improvement. Leading is helping, coaching, and supporting, not threatening, ranking, or punishing (See Appendix 4).

Because of this, administrators and other school leaders are essential players in initiating and maintaining the transformation process required to build Schools of Quality. And, because the journey is never-ending, school leaders must be enabled and supported by all of the school's stakeholders in their continuing efforts to make the school better and better, day by day, year by year.

# 5

# Getting Started

I f you are considering initiating a Total Quality transformation process in your school or district, you're probably wondering where you should start. There are many good pathways to building Schools of Quality. It is important that you craft one specifically for your own special circumstances, taking into account the primary needs and wants of your suppliers and customers in the school system and community. Your work will necessarily be based upon your community's unique culture, history, and demographic and socioeconomic make-up and trends. These are the first and most important considerations when beginning any Total Quality process.

School leaders who are successfully applying Total Quality Management principles and practices to create Schools of Quality have shared some helpful hints with me that you may find useful in developing a customized culture of continuous improvement for your school system:

• Learn as much as possible about Total Quality Management and its applications to education. Before you try to make TQM a part of your school system's everyday functioning, immerse yourself in the growing body of literature on TQM as it applies to education as well as to the business world. It may be helpful to attend TQM workshops and conferences, especially those presented by fellow educators who can effectively translate business-oriented TQM philosophies for use in education organizations. You may also want to join organizations focused on Total Quality, such as ASCD's TQM-Education Network.

Take time to discuss your Total Quality ideas with corporate leaders in your community to get business perspectives on the Total Quality movement and local companies' continuous improvement processes. You might also find it useful to bring in an education-focused consultant to help you and other school leaders think through some of the thornier issues you will confront when you begin the Total Quality transformation process. Learn how to use the Tools of TQM (see appendix 1), understanding that these tools don't constitute the process of transformation, but they do provide ways of gathering and analyzing the necessary information for optimizing systems.

• Make a personal commitment to Total Quality and *kaizen* for yourself, your family, your schools, and your community. When you make your life a constant example of the journey toward Total Quality, you establish yourself as a role model for others in your community and schools. Demonstrate TQM leadership to staff members, associates, students, parents, and the entire community by "talking your walk and walking your talk." This shows everyone that your new commitment to the Total Quality transformation process isn't simply another "flavor of the month," but rather a long-term philosophy of life. Those around you will begin to see the benefits of applying Total Quality principles and will begin to think about how Total Quality relates to their own lives. When Total Quality permeates a community's thinking, the result is the establishment of a true "learning community" dedicated to the principle of *kaizen* in every aspect of life, including the work of young people and educators in all of the community's schools.

• Provide leadership by building networks of support **for the transformation.** Many school leaders have found it helpful to form a school-community Quality Council to determine needs and broad systemic goals, and to enlist the active support of all sectors of the community in accomplishing a Total Quality transformation. Representatives of all customer and supplier groups (internal and external) should be involved in the development of your schools' vision, mission, goals, principles, measures, and overall strategic plan. Crucial to the success of this process is partnership with local teacher organizations who should be co-creators of the Total Quality transformation from the very beginning. Teachers, custodians, cafeteria workers, secretaries, administrators, parents, and students must be effectively represented if strong networks of support are to be created. The traditional fear-ridden Tayloresque environment of compliance, control, and command must be replaced by an environment of encouragement, nurturing, and collegiality.

• Build awareness of TQM throughout your organization and the community. Use every opportunity to spread the news of the ongoing Total Quality transformation. In this neverending process, educators must teach young people and the entire community about the principles and practices of Total Quality, and support its implementation in all facets of community life. Your schools can, in time, become centers for modelling and teaching TQM to the entire community.

Instead of providing the media with symbolic numbers to demonstrate students' progress, you might provide local newspapers and TV stations with opportunities to observe and interview students who are demonstrating their real-life achievements in the schools and in the community. If your community has cable TV, utilize the public access channel to broadcast programs celebrating the ongoing processes of continuous improvement that are at the heart of your schools' and community's Total Quality transformation. It's much more effective for the people of the community to see with their own eyes the good things happening in their schools than to read published "box scores" comparing standardized test results of neighboring school districts.

• Create a resource base to support the time and training necessary to make the transformation a long-term success. Make no mistake about it, a Total Quality culture in schools and communities cannot be created overnight. Effective, ongoing communication and teamwork will require investments of time (apart from classroom time) by teachers, administrators, and others. Training is an absolute *must*. Outside sources of information and facilitation will cost money and time, but we know that whatever expenditures are made at the front end of the transformation process will be repaid many times over as students become more successful in their school work, teachers and administrators work together more smoothly and effectively, and the community observes very real gains in student achievement.

• Assess the needs of customers and suppliers throughout your school and in your community. Who *are* your suppliers and customers, internal and external, primary and secondary? What are their needs, expressed and unspoken? How can your efforts result in processes and systems better designed to build quality into the work everyone performs together, resulting in continuously improving customer satisfaction? Focus groups, surveys, brainstorming sessions, nominal group techniques, and other processes can help you gather data you will need to determine their needs and desires. Particular attention must be given to shifting demographic trends during the process of charting present and future needs. Work with childcare and social welfare agencies, lawmakers, and effective parenting groups to develop Total Quality community support environments conducive to the fullest development of your Schools of Quality. Extend your outreach efforts to all internal customers and suppliers within your organization. By building cross-disciplinary, multi-level teams of teachers, administrators, classified employees, parents, and students, you will be able to gather data that represent the widest possible range of customer/supplier perceptions and needs.

• Benchmark your system, its processes, and its outcomes. Benchmarking is the process of scouting other organizations to identify the Total Quality systems and processes that your organization may want to emulate or adapt to your own local needs. How does your system compare with others? What could you, your customers, and your suppliers learn from other schools and communities?

Remember when copying meant cheating? Today, in the cooperative learning classroom, as well as in institutional improvement processes, people are encouraged to search for standard bearers in their fields, learn from them, and apply their learnings to the continuous improvement of their own work and the work of their organizations. Using the TQM tools and techniques found in Appendix 1, you and your Quality Council may want to collect information from schools, companies, hospitals, and other organizations through on-site visits. Information can also be collected by phone and mail, through a search of the literature, and from outside consultants.

• Use the continuous improvement process on the processes and outcomes of your system. Start with a relatively small part of your system. Use the PDSA Cycle (or Juran's Spiral or the Experience Pattern Spiral) to delineate your continuous improvement process. Gather feedback information from customers and suppliers and use this feedback to constantly modify your systems and processes. This approach will be helpful for everyone throughout the school system, including students learning how to monitor their own educational processes, bus drivers trying to reduce the time variations of their bus runs, administrators seeking outside funding for school projects, teachers planning new initiatives to support greater student successes, and parents and other people of the community supporting their schools' continuous improvement processes. The applications of the continuous improvement process, as you will discover, are as endless as the Total Quality journey itself.

• Celebrate all successes, even small ones. Successful Total Quality transformation efforts invariably recognize incremental improvements, especially by teams, and celebrate them in collaborative, noncompetitive environments. In the classroom, teachers and students share sincere celebrations of improvements in effort as well as results with administrators and parents often joining in. Teacher teams are also recognized by their peers, administrators, and parents for their ongoing successes. Causes for celebrating improved efforts and achievements abound in Schools of Quality, limited only by the constraints of the imagination and by vestiges of Tayloresque management practices.

• Tie compatible existing educational philosophies and practices together under the TQM umbrella. Many school leaders have found that contemporary concepts and practices—site-based management, teaming, interdisciplinary courses, whole language, authentic assessment, mastery learning, and the effective schools research, to name a few—can easily be united under the Total Quality umbrella. When TQM and continuous improvement become unifying factors, these compatible components become part of an ongoing philosophy of commitment to improvement with roots that should grow deeper as time goes on.

• Make your journey to Total Quality a slow and steady process. The TQM transformation takes time. Avoid the temptation to plunge into it expecting your schools and community to achieve Total Quality status within a year or two. In most cases it takes at least two to three years of constant commitment and hard work to redesign suboptimizing systems and processes, and another two years to see tangible, longlasting benefits. Spread the word to avoid the damaging effects of cynicism.

• Approach your Total Quality transformation with patience, forgiveness, and a helping hand. Total Quality is a journey, not a destination. To make the journey one that keeps getting better and better, everyone (especially school leaders) must be patient. The creation of Schools of Quality requires dramatic changes in the way people live and work. Change initially brings uncertainty, and oftentimes resentment. Old wounds may be reopened, and recriminations exchanged. The mixture of apprehension and exuberance with which many "front-line workers" initially greet their new decision-making powers often turns to frustration and cynicism when some of those decisions don't pan out. People who previously had little decision-making authority need time to learn how to use TQM tools, principles, and practices. Training in effective modes of active listening, win-win discussion, and group problem-solving techniques will prove to be very solid investments in the long-term results of your Total Quality transformation.

Through the rough spots, it will be important to remember that the overarching reason for your efforts is to enable your own continuous growth and improvement and that of the people with whom you work and live. Getting better and better, day by day. *Kaizen*.

Reflecting upon his experiences implementing the widely-known experiment in continuous improvement at Mt. Edgecumbe High School in Sitka, Alaska, Superintendent Larrae Rocheleau advises that a "general amnesty" be declared and respected by everyone in the system. Forgiveness of everybody's past offenses is crucial when developing a new collaborative, team-focused TQM approach to replace outmoded authoritarian management modes.

And finally:

• Don't be afraid to fail. Schools of Quality, as well as other Total Quality organizations, are places where it's safe to take risks, okay to fail on the way to successes. Failures are viewed as a natural part of life's explorations, an inherent characteristic of the continuous improvement journey. Encourage the creation and expression of new ideas from the classroom to the principal's office to the school board conference room, and into the larger community. As you begin your endless journey toward Total Quality, bear in mind and share one of my favorite sentiments (shown on page 50), "Don't Be Afraid To Fail," which United Technologies ran as a full-page ad in the *Wall Street Journal* (1981) more than a decade ago.

# Don't Be Afraid To Fail

You've failed many times, although you may not remember. You fell down the first time you tried to walk. You almost drowned the first time you tried to swim, didn't you? Did you hit the ball the first time you swung a bat?

Heavy hitters, the ones who hit the most home runs, also strike out a lot.

R.H. Macy failed seven times before his store in New York caught on. English novelist John Creasy got 753 rejection slips before he published 564 books. Babe Ruth struck out 1,330 times, but he also hit 714 home runs. Don't worry about failure.

Worry about chances you miss when you don't even try.

# APPENDIX 1
## Tools for the Transformation

In the process of transforming their organizations into Total Quality learning organizations, leaders in business, education, and other spheres have found it helpful to use TQM tools and techniques to better perceive, collect, analyze, and understand relevant data. This appendix takes a brief look at the TQM tools that are most useful for educators in their schools' journey of continuous improvement.

First, a word of caution and clarification. As Marshall Sashkin and Kenneth Kiser (1983) have warned: "The tools are not TQM." Tools and techniques, they stress, are useful but "not sufficient for 'TQM.' When made the focus of TQM, tools and techniques can even prevent the organization from taking the additional steps needed for TQM. In this way, an overemphasis on tools, in the mistaken belief that the tools are TQM, can lead the organization in the opposite direction, away from an organizational commitment to quality."

## The Seven Traditional Tools

We will start with the Seven Traditional Tools, as they are known by practitioners of TQM. An application for schools is provided for each tool.

### Tool 1: The Flow Chart
#### Detailed Flow Chart

The Flow Chart is a diagram of the steps in a process, shown in their natural sequence. By showing how a process works in practice, potential difficulties can be identified and short-circuited, resulting in the creation of a new, improved process. This tool is useful in the process of thinking through a new process before it is implemented so that potential pitfalls can be more easily avoided.

In the following example (see page 52), a state school boards association used this Detailed Flow Chart to diagram the sequence of its strategic vision and planning process. This chart shows the developmental stages of the organization's vision, mission statement, goals and objectives, strategies, and action plan.

The process of creating this flow chart resulted in better communication and greater buy-in by all persons involved in the process of school transformation. Because all of the steps in this process were clear from the outset, the statewide transformation began with a much better chance for long-term success.

# DETAILED FLOW CHART

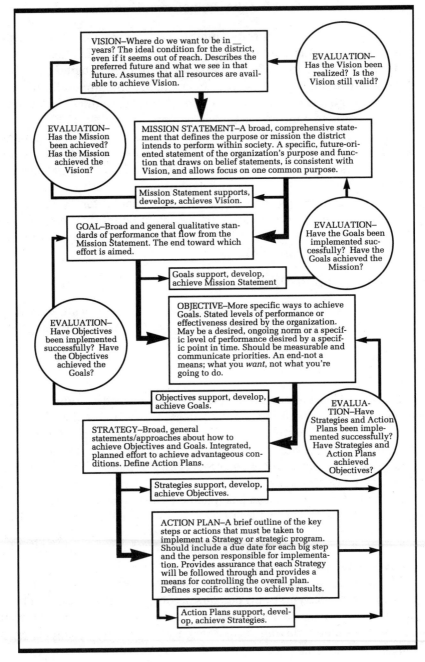

VISION–Where do we want to be in ___ years? The ideal condition for the district, even if it seems out of reach. Describes the preferred future and what we see in that future. Assumes that all resources are available to achieve Vision.

EVALUATION– Has the Vision been realized? Is the Vision still valid?

EVALUATION– Has the Mission been achieved? Has the Mission achieved the Vision?

MISSION STATEMENT–A broad, comprehensive statement that defines the purpose or mission the district intends to perform within society. A specific, future-oriented statement of the organization's purpose and function that draws on belief statements, is consistent with Vision, and allows focus on one common purpose.

Mission Statement supports, develops, achieves Vision.

GOAL–Broad and general qualitative standards of performance that flow from the Mission Statement. The end toward which effort is aimed.

EVALUATION– Have the Goals been implemented successfully? Have the Goals achieved the Mission?

Goals support, develop, achieve Mission Statement

OBJECTIVE–More specific ways to achieve Goals. Stated levels of performance or effectiveness desired by the organization. May be a desired, ongoing norm or a specific level of performance desired by a specific point in time. Should be measurable and communicate priorities. An end-not a means; what you *want*, not what you're going to do.

EVALUATION– Have Objectives been implemented successfully? Have the Objectives achieved the Goals?

Objectives support, develop, achieve Goals.

EVALUA-TION–Have Strategies and Action Plans been implemented successfully? Have Strategies and Action Plans achieved Objectives?

STRATEGY–Broad, general statements/approaches about how to achieve Objectives and Goals. Integrated, planned effort to achieve advantageous conditions. Define Action Plans.

Strategies support, develop, achieve Objectives.

ACTION PLAN–A brief outline of the key steps or actions that must be taken to implement a Strategy or strategic program. Should include a due date for each big step and the person responsible for implementation. Provides assurance that each Strategy will be followed through and provides a means for controlling the overall plan. Defines specific actions to achieve results.

Action Plans support, develop, achieve Strategies.

Here is another example of a Detailed Flow Chart, showing the steps in a school's attendance process. An administration-teacher team used this tool to understand the existing process so their improvement efforts could be based upon a full understanding of current practices.

# DETAILED FLOW CHART

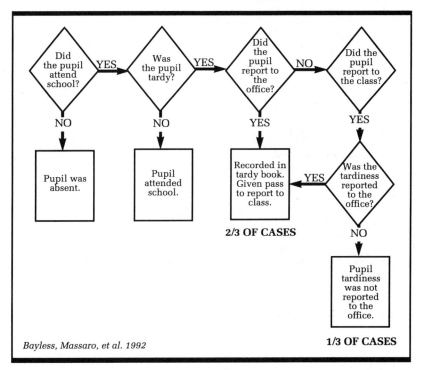

Bayless, Massaro, et al. 1992

## *Top-Down Flow Chart*

Another type of flow chart, the Top-Down Flow Chart, has many applications to education. Students can use it to analyze their learning processes, identifying those steps that need more time and effort, or perhaps a different approach. Interdisciplinary teacher teams can use the flow chart to map out a new interactive process for cross-disciplinary instruction. School boards can use it to plan construction of new school facilities or the implementation of new policies.

In the following example, a team of teachers and school leaders used a Top-Down Flow Chart to identify the steps they needed to take together in order to implement a Total Quality transformation in their school district.

## TOP-DOWN FLOW CHART

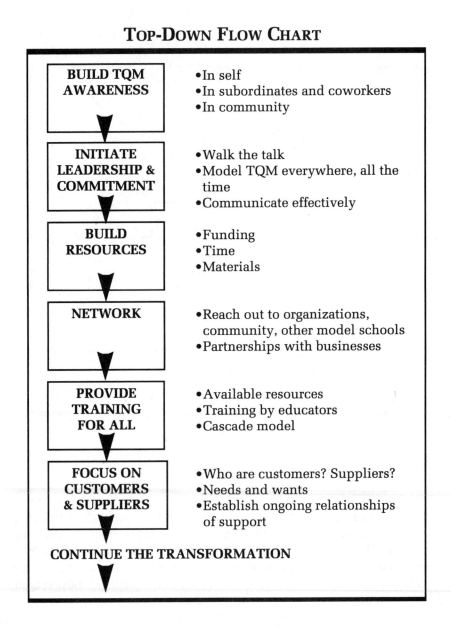

| | |
|---|---|
| **BUILD TQM AWARENESS** | •In self<br>•In subordinates and coworkers<br>•In community |
| **INITIATE LEADERSHIP & COMMITMENT** | •Walk the talk<br>•Model TQM everywhere, all the time<br>•Communicate effectively |
| **BUILD RESOURCES** | •Funding<br>•Time<br>•Materials |
| **NETWORK** | •Reach out to organizations, community, other model schools<br>•Partnerships with businesses |
| **PROVIDE TRAINING FOR ALL** | •Available resources<br>•Training by educators<br>•Cascade model |
| **FOCUS ON CUSTOMERS & SUPPLIERS** | •Who are customers? Suppliers?<br>•Needs and wants<br>•Establish ongoing relationships of support |

**CONTINUE THE TRANSFORMATION**

The process of creating this Flow Chart *as a team* resulted in greater buy-in by everyone involved in the transformation process. Because all of the team members felt a part of the process from the outset, the transformation began with a much better chance for long-term success.[1]

## Tool 2: The Fishbone Diagram

This tool, called the Fishbone because of its shape, is also known as the Cause-and-Effect diagram or the Ishikawa diagram, after its creator, Kaoru Ishikawa. The Fishbone, shown on p. 56, is helpful in determining the root causes and effects within an organization's processes and systems. It is a modification of the "process arrow" diagram discussed in Chapter 3.

The Fishbone can be used to identify factors in the process responsible for an existing problem or to plan a process more effectively, so that inputs result in the desired outcomes.

To use the Fishbone to uncover the causes of an existing problem, first write the outcome problem or condition you want to study in the "head" of the fish, on the right. Then, on the big "bones" of the fish, list the major factors possibly responsible for the outcome. On the little bones, write the factors that possibly contribute to, or modify, the major factors that ultimately lead to the current outcome.

The fishbone on page 56 is used to analyze a school problem: bus runs arriving late. In this example, despite everyone's best intentions and efforts, several bus runs had been arriving late every day at a particular school. This has resulted in some students coming into their 1st period classes as much as twenty minutes late. The school administration created a team consisting of parents, students, bus drivers, the transportation supervisor, and the school's vice principal to study the problem and come up with possible solutions. To collect and analyze data relevant to this dilemma, they used a Fishbone diagram.

Notice that, after listing the factors they considered most significant on the "skeleton," the team circled those factors having the strongest impact on the problem: the length of some bus routes, the age of the buses, and the number of students and stops on each bus route. The team found that some bus routes required the pick-up of nearly twice the number of students on other routes, and that those bus runs took an

---

[1]See Peter Scholtes, et al., The Team Handbook for more about Detailed and Top-Down Flow Charts.

# FISHBONE DIAGRAM

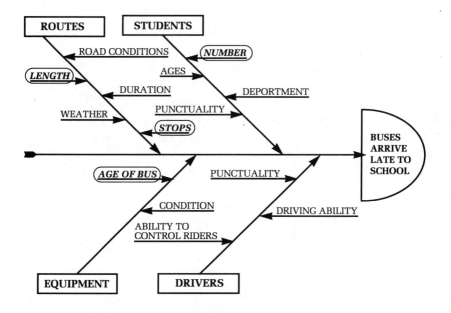

average of 60 percent longer than the shortest bus runs. Also, the oldest buses were being used for the longer routes.

Using the data they collected, the team petitioned the school board for several new bus runs. Once the new runs were established, all of the bus runs arrived at school well before the beginning of first period. Problem solved!

The Fishbone can also be used to plan an improvement process. When a quality circle S-Team of students used the Fishbone to plan ways of improving their school work, they came up with the data in the completed Fishbone Diagram on page 57.

The student team determined that a more attractive school environment, improved relationships with teachers, increased support by parents and families, and some extra assistance from members of their S-Team would help them improve their learning processes, energizing them to make better grades and to achieve the "greatest possible success" in their classes. Based upon the data, the student team organized other students into a committee to clean up and improve the appearance of

# FISHBONE DIAGRAM

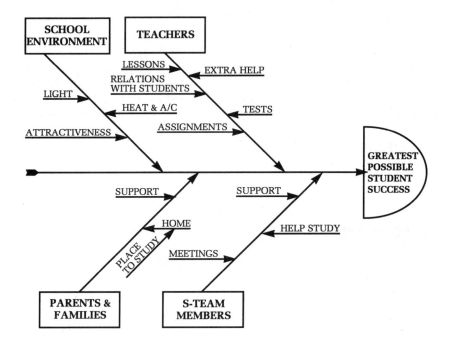

the school campus; they began to work more closely with their teachers to improve the effectiveness of their interactions inside and outside of the classroom; and they talked with their family members to create times and spaces within their homes that would be more conducive to effective studying. The students also agreed to meet once a week in their S-Teams to give additional help and support to one other in their own continuous improvement and learning processes. This plan resulted in better grades for all of the team's members, enhanced pride and joy in their work, and a greater feeling of belonging and shared caring.

### Tool 3: Pareto Chart

The Pareto Chart is named after the 19th century Italian economist Vilfredo Pareto, whose research was used by Joseph Juran in formulating what he called the Pareto Principle: Relatively few *vital* factors (as little as 20%) are responsible for the vast majority (as much as 80%) of all problems in any process or system. The lesson of the Pareto Principle is this: Analyze your information carefully, so you can identify the *vital few* factors that require attention first and foremost. The Pareto Chart is a bar chart in which factors in a process are shown in descending order of importance or frequency of occurrence.

The following Pareto Chart was used by an administration-teacher team to study the types of student disruptions in their classes. Finding that the vast majority of all disruption problems came from students talking in class, they focused their attention on this factor, instituting student training and more interactive teaching/learning styles-oriented instruction that capitalizes on the students' desire to communicate with each other in class. This resulted in a dramatic decrease in class disruptions.

## PARETO CHART

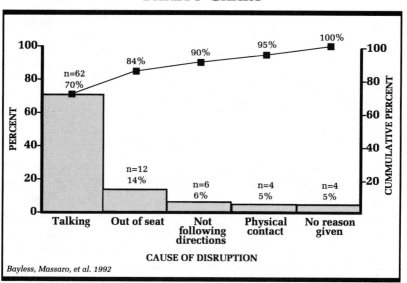

Bayless, Massaro, et al. 1992

## Tool 4: The Scatter Diagram

The Scatter Diagram is a tool used to analyze the correlation between two variables. It can be used to identify possible cause-effect relationships between factors in a process. In the Scatter Diagram, the measures of one factor are shown on the horizontal axis, while measures of the other factor are shown on the vertical axis. If there is a positive correlation between the two factors, indicating a possible cause-effect relationship, the direction of the cluster of points will show a directional design from lower left to upper right. Any other pattern indicates the absence of a positive correlation between the two factors, thus putting into doubt the existence of a cause-effect relationship.

In the following example, a student was taught how to use the Scatter Diagram to analyze the relationship between hours spent studying and test grades.

By using the Scatter Diagram, the student was convinced that there is a positive correlation between study time and test grades.

## SCATTER DIAGRAM

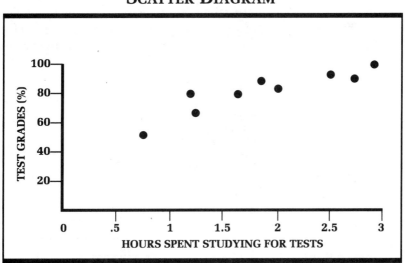

## Tool 5: The PDSA Cycle

The Plan-Do-Study Act Cycle invented by Walter Shewhart and developed by W. Edwards Deming is a useful tool for carrying on a continuous improvement process. The PDSA Cycle is a model of the way people learn, so it can help us analyze and improve the processes we use in getting a job done.

Students can be taught to use the PDSA Cycle to better understand the systemic nature of their own learning processes. Here is an example of a PDSA Cycle developed by a student.

In this example, the student plans how to approach the work of the new unit (in the "Plan" step). Then the student does the work of the unit (the "Do" step), taking notes, doing the required and suggested reading, participating in class, doing assignments including the unit project, and taking the unit test. All the while, the student keeps a journal, reflecting on the processes chosen to accomplish all the tasks of the unit.

At the end of the unit, the student and teacher collaboratively study the processes they used to accomplish the goals of the unit (the "Study" step). Using the student's journal and all of the work done by the student, they examine what went right and what should be improved in their work together in the next unit.

Then, in the "Act" step, the student and teacher use what they have learned in this process to improve the ways the next unit is done. Thus, the PDSA Cycle becomes a vehicle for teachers and students to continu-

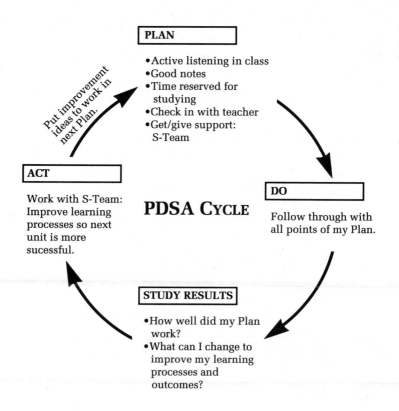

PLAN
- Active listening in class
- Good notes
- Time reserved for studying
- Check in with teacher
- Get/give support: S-Team

Put improvement ideas to work in next Plan.

ACT
Work with S-Team: Improve learning processes so next unit is more sucessful.

**PDSA CYCLE**

DO
Follow through with all points of my Plan.

STUDY RESULTS
- How well did my Plan work?
- What can I change to improve my learning processes and outcomes?

ously improve their collaborative efforts to create better and better ways of interacting with each other, toward greater and greater successes.

The PDSA Cycle is one of the most versatile tools of TQM. It can be used to study and improve virtually any process, from conducting effective and efficient faculty meetings and school board sessions, to planning field trips, to conducting community and customer surveys, to attracting more parents and business people to support the work of the school.

### Tool 6: The Histogram

The Histogram is a bar chart representation of the spread or dispersion of variable data. Histograms tend to show a natural distribution toward the center prior to intervention. An example for schools is the bell curve, showing a natural clustering of grades in a pretest before the beginning of the unit (or instructional intervention) as shown here:

## HISTOGRAM

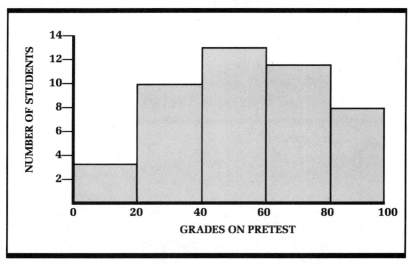

Please note: It is neither natural nor desirable to have grades *at the unit's end* conform to the normal distribution of a bell curve. If the pretest does not show a normal distribution, further analysis is needed to determine whether there are special causes or common causes of variation—helpful data in determining how best to teach the unit.

### Tool 7: The Control Chart

The Control Chart (sometimes called the Statistical Control Chart) is used to display graphically the variation in an ongoing process. This tool, invented by Walter Shewhart, began the statistical process control movement, which was the precursor of the Total Quality Management movement in industry and education.

The Control Chart has a horizontal axis for tracking time and a vertical axis for tracking the system or process under consideration. If the process goes outside the upper or lower control limits, it is considered "out of statistical control." In such cases, the system should be adjusted to bring the process back into control.

Let's say the optimum temperature for a school building is 72 degrees, and that the upper and lower control limits of your heating system have been plotted at 76 and 66 degrees. This is the normal variation, within the constraints of your present system. To decrease the 11 point spread, your system must be changed. If the temperature goes outside that range, you need to determine whether the reason is a special cause of variation, or a common cause, and take appropriate actions.

The procedure for using a Control Chart is rather sophisticated, and may require further research and the services of a professional statistician.

## CONTROL CHART

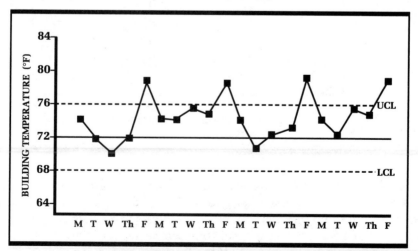

## Newer Tools

In addition to the Seven Traditional Tools, newer TQM tools for planning and problem solving are being developed as new needs arise. Here are a few of the newer tools and some of their applications to education.

### Tool 8: The Affinity Diagram

The Affinity Diagram method, developed by Kawakita Jiro, is a simple categorization process, putting together chosen factors that have a natural link with one another. The Affinity Diagram is often a preliminary step before using the Fishbone Diagram. Take another look at the Top-Down Flow Chart example. This is an Affinity Diagram that might have been designed before that was created.

Notice that the major headings under the title of the Affinity Diagram provide the context for the factors written in the Top-Down Flow Chart.

## AFFINITY DIAGRAM

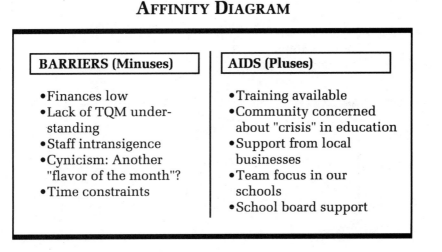

| BARRIERS (Minuses) | AIDS (Pluses) |
|---|---|
| •Finances low<br>•Lack of TQM understanding<br>•Staff intransigence<br>•Cynicism: Another "flavor of the month"?<br>•Time constraints | •Training available<br>•Community concerned about "crisis" in education<br>•Support from local businesses<br>•Team focus in our schools<br>•School board support |

63

### Tool 9: The Force Field

The Force Field, or Barriers-and-Aids Chart, developed by Kurt Lewin (1948), provides a method for identifying the factors opposing change and those pushing for change. By weighing the factors on both sides, and effectively counterbalancing the negative factors, it is possible to develop an action plan with a great chance of succeeding in the long run.

Here is a Force Field showing some barriers and aids in the implementation of a districtwide Total Quality transformation process.

## FORCE FIELD

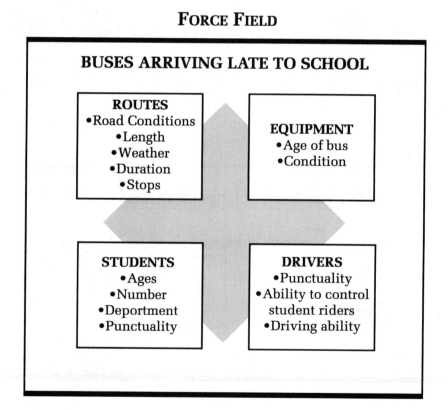

## Tool 10: The Five Whys

Uncovering the real reasons behind a problem often requires a process that goes deeper than simply answering the question "Why?" A Japanese tradition suggests that only after answering that question five times will the true causes of a problem begin to emerge. Here is an example:

1. Why didn't you do your homework last night?
    I didn't have time to do my homework.
2. Why didn't you have time to do your homework?
    I had other things I had to do.
3. Why did you have other things to do?
    I had to be with my little brother.
4. Why did you have to be with your little brother?
    Because there was no one else at home.
5. Why was there no one else at home?
    Because my parents went to a party and my little brother started throwing up right after they left. I had to take care of him until my parents got home after midnight, and then I was too tired to do my homework. If it's okay with you, I'll hand it in tomorrow.

## Tool 11: Cross-Impact Matrix

A Cross-Impact Matrix (CIM) is a tool used to analyze the impact, or effect, of a certain factor upon a specific area of consequence. The simplest kind of CIM is a table of horizontal and vertical columns. At the beginning of each horizontal row, one of a set of related factors is given. At the top of each column, specific areas of consequence are listed. Each factor in a row is matched with each area of consequence listed in a column, one at a time. The matching of factors and areas of consequence raises the question: What impact do factors and areas of consequence have on each other?

Here is an example of a CIM designed to help students consider the various possible effects of drug use. As students fill in the matrix, they become more and more aware of the wide scope of personal repercussions if they choose to abuse drugs.

# CROSS-IMPACT MATRIX

| PERSONAL DECISIONS ABOUT DRUG USE | | | | | | |
|---|---|---|---|---|---|---|
| | Relations With My Parents | Peer Relationships | My Body | My Mind | Financial Situation | My Education |
| Tobacco | Ⓖ 1 S My parents do not approve of using tobacco. | Ⓖ 2 S My peers think using tobacco is obnoxious. | Ⓖ 3 S Cardiovascular & respiratory problems result. | G 4 Ⓢ Tobacco is not known to be a mind-altering drug. | G 5 S | G 6 S |
| Alcohol | G 7 S | G 8 S | G 9 S | G 10 S | G 11 S | G 12 S |
| Marijuana | G 13 S | G 14 S | G 15 S | G 16 S | G 17 S | G 18 S |
| PCP | G 19 S | G 20 S | G 21 S | G 22 S | G 23 S | G 24 S |
| Cocaine | G 25 S | G 26 S | G 27 S | G 28 S | G 29 S | G 30 S |
| Heroin | G 31 S | G 32 S | G 33 S | G 34 S | G 35 S | G 36 S |

G=GREAT IMPACT    S=SMALL IMPACT          *Bonstingl 1991*

## Tool 12: The Decision Wheel

The Decision Wheel (sometimes called the Ripple Effect Diagram) is a tool for thinking through the probable effects of actions taken. The decision or action to be studied is written in the center bubble. The actual or probable effects of the central action are written in the four bubbles of the first circle surrounding the central action. Then, in the bubbles of the second circle, the actual and probable effects of the first circle's effects are described. The Decision Wheel shows graphically the effects, often unintended, of our actions.

Here is a Decision Wheel completed by a students whose S-Team decided to collect canned food for their community's soup kitchen. Through their work with this Decision Wheel, they gained a fuller appreciation of the ripple effects of their efforts.

# DECISION WHEEL

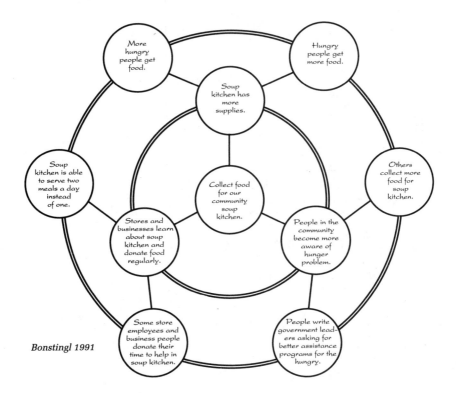

Bonstingl 1991

67

**Tool 13: The Checksheet**

Checksheets are a well-known device for recording data. Necessary information about the characteristics of a process or a product can be recorded by simply making a check mark. Checksheets are particularly useful in spotting omissions that may be detrimental to the success of a process.

Here is an example of a checksheet that might be used in the process of preparing for a faculty meeting.

## CHECKSHEET

| CHECKLIST FOR FACULTY MEETING | | |
|---|---|---|
| **ITEM** | **YES** | **NO** |
| 1. Agenda Handouts | √ | |
| 2. Business cards for all faculty members | √ | |
| 3. Get well card for R.J. | √ | |
| 4. Articles on TQM in education | √ | |
| 5. New Board Policy | √ | |
| 6. Inservice courses | √ | |

These are only a few of the many TQM tools and techniques available for use in the Total Quality transformation process. Brainstorming, nominal group techniques, benchmarking, customer/ supplier surveys and questionnaires, and other methods of getting, arranging, and analyzing data can also be helpful in your Quality journey.

Once again, it is good to remember that however useful these tools may be in the process of continuous improvement, they are not the transformative process itself, and should not be considered the heart and soul of the process. To place such importance on the tools is to potentially deny the importance of the people who are at the heart of every transformative process, including that of Total Quality Management.

# APPENDIX 2:
## THE FOUR PILLARS OF SCHOOLS OF QUALITY—ROLES OF STAKEHOLDER-PARTICIPANTS
### PILLAR #1:
### A CUSTOMER-SUPPLIER FOCUS

| | |
|---|---|
| **Policy-makers** | Customers of school leaders and those they serve, including students, teachers, administrators, parents and families, and other stakeholders in the community's schools. |
| | Suppliers of policies designed to facilitate the optimization of the entire system, permitting students and teachers as the school's front-line workers, to maximize everyone's potentials through a constant focus on process-oriented continuous improvement. |
| **School Leaders** | Customers of families who send their children to the school, of vendors who supply the school with necessities, and of state and federal agencies that create legal contexts for schools. |
| | Suppliers of effective fear-free environments and policies that benefit all contributors to the continuous improvement of the school and its people. |
| **Teachers** | Customers of families who send their children to school, of administration and school board policies, and of other teachers who work with the same students. |
| | Suppliers of supportive mentoring to students, helping them in a wide variety of ways to continuously improve their character, competency, and compassion. |

| | |
|---|---|
| **Students** | Customers of efforts by teachers, administrators, and support staff who provide environments and services conducive to the students' continuous improvement.<br><br>Suppliers of consistent effort toward their own continuous improvement and that of others at school, at home, and in the community. |
| **Parents and Families** | Customers of the school's total effort on behalf of their children.<br><br>Suppliers of pre- and post-natal physical and psychological support to help maximize their children's opportunities for growth and development of innate intelligences. Suppliers of consistent personal involvement in support of the school and its people. |
| **Business People** | Customers of the school's total effort toward the maximization of successes by students and teachers in their work together.<br><br>Suppliers of financial and in-kind support, and opportunities for teachers, students, and others in the school and community to learn about continuous improvement from a business point of view. |
| **Community Members** | Customers of the school in terms of continuing opportunities to learn, to contribute to community improvement, and to leave a legacy for coming generations.<br><br>Suppliers of financial and psychological support for the continuous improvement of the school and its people. Good schools need more than tax monies. They need the active support of everyone, even citizens without school children. |

# APPENDIX 2, CONTINUED

## PILLAR #2:
## DEDICATION TO CONTINUOUS IMPROVEMENT (*KAIZEN*)

| | |
|---|---|
| **Policy-makers** | Demonstrate constant dedication to continuous improvement of self and others at home, at work, and in the community. Create policies to build fear-free learning environments, systems, and processes most conducive to *kaizen* and the creation of a "yearning for learning" among students, teachers, school leaders, and all the people of the school and community. |
| **School Leaders** | Demonstrate constant dedication to continuous improvement of self and others at home, at work, and in the community. Help policy-makers to create policies to build fear-free learning environments, systems, and processes most conducive to kaizen and the creation of a "yearning for learning" among students, teachers, school leaders, and all the people of the school and community. |
| **Teachers** | Demonstrate constant dedication to continuous improvement of self and others at home, at school, and in the community. Create fear-free classroom environments and learning processes that help students identify and constantly develop their wide range of innate abilities. Show young people how to learn and share with others, helping everyone to grow and improve every day. Help students create within themselves an unquenchable "yearning for learning," developing the tools required to learn and grow. |

| | |
|---|---|
| **Students** | Demonstrate constant dedication to continuous improvement of self and others at home, at school, and in the community. Develop the courage to improve character, competence, and compassion more and more fully every day. Seek and maximize opportunities for lifelong and life-wide learning, in and out of school, for self and others. |
| **Parents and Families** | Demonstrate constant dedication to continuous improvement of self and others at home, at work, and in the community. Provide children and other family members with real-life role models who love to learn and who build active relationships of unconditional love and mutual respect for everyone in the family, knowing that such relationships are the fertile ground of continuous growth and improvement of character, competence, and compassion. |
| **Business People** | Demonstrate constant dedication to continuous improvement of self and others at home, at work, and in the community. At work, help build a fear-free company culture based upon trust, respect, and mutual dedication to everyone's continuing growth and development. Know that growth of the bottom line is less important than the growth of the one true resource that makes a consistently healthy bottom line possible: people, especially the young. Develop a Total Quality culture in which the school's graduates can continue to learn, grow, and nourish themselves and others as employees. |
| **Community Members** | Demonstrate constant dedication to continuous improvement of self and others at home, at work, and in the community, particularly in full support of the school and its people. This dedication is shown by vocal and financial support to fully fund school efforts and a communitywide dedication to lifelong and life-wide *kaizen* learning for all. |

| | |
|---|---|
| **Policy-makers** | Create policies that design quality into the system and its processes from the very beginning. Work from the start with the educators who will implement the policies, learning from their experience at the front lines. |
| **School Leaders** | Build quality into the system and its many interlinking processes. See things gone wrong as opportunities to fix the system rather than to fix blame on individuals. The health of relationships within the system must be given priority over short-term symbols of the system's outcomes. |
| **Teachers** | Build quality into the system of teaching and learning. Create learning opportunities that connect with students' other real-life experience—the larger life-system of which schooling is one of many processes. As integral elements of the students' personal learning systems, teachers work with students to constantly fine-tune their ongoing work processes so that successive units of study can be learned with greater and greater mastery. |

| | |
|---|---|
| **Students** | Build quality into personal learning systems. Focus on connections between what school teaches and what other real-life experiences teach. Concentrate on ways of improving character, competence, and compassion in self and others, which results in continuous improvement in a wide range of efforts. |
| **Parents and Families** | Help students and teachers build quality into their work together by emphasizing children's learning processes, not just grades and other short-term indicators of learning programs. Use voice and vote to support systems and processes of continuous learning for everyone in the community—especially young people. Combine efforts with other people in the system to create synergistic progress. |
| **Business People** | Build quality into systems and processes. Offer insights to the school and its people, sharing successes and providing support to employees. Stress the systemic nature of continuous improvement in the world of business, and foster such efforts in the school. Help develop partnerships with the school and its people, for everyone's long-term benefit. |
| **Community Members** | Support the school's systemic and process-oriented transformations in teaching and learning. Know that simplistic numerical symbols of students' performances are not adequate indicators of the health of learning systems and processes within the school. Communicate this knowledge to the media. |

## PILLAR #4:

# MANAGEMENT'S CONSTANT DEDICATION TO TOTAL QUALITY

| | |
|---|---|
| **Policy-makers** | Create policies that encourage a constant dedication to Total Quality by everyone within the system, and by everyone impacted by the system. |
| **School Leaders** | "Quality cannot be delegated," states W. Edwards Deming. Only management can initiate organizational cultures of quality. Workers, acting alone, cannot do it. School leaders must "talk their walk and walk their talk" in everything they do, if Total Quality is to eventually permeate all aspects of the school and its community. There are no quick fixes or magic bullets. TQM is not a flavor of the month, and must be developed through teamwork, with deliberation, over the span of years. |
| **Teachers** | |
| **Students** | Everyone in the school and the community must be supportive of the changes school leaders must make |
| **Parents and Families** | in the process of transforming schools into Schools of Quality. Changes bring pleasures and pains. |
| **Business People** | Everyone must be ready to experience both, over time, with patience and dedication, if Total Quality is to |
| **Community Members** | inform the deep culture of the school and its community. |

# APPENDIX 3

## Deming's Fourteen Points Applied to Companies and Schools

*The following represents the author's interpretation of The Fourteen Points developed by Dr. W. Edwards Deming, internationally renowned authority in the field of statistical quality control.*

| POINT | COMPANIES | SCHOOLS |
|---|---|---|
| 1 Create constancy of purpose for improvement of product and service. | Company must focus on staying in business and providing jobs through research, innovation, and continual improvement of products and services. Maximization of profits is less important than this focus. | School must focus on helping students to maximize their own potentials through continuous improvement of teachers' and students' work together. Maximization of test scores and assessment symbols is less important than the progress inherent in the continuous learning process of each student. |
| 2 Adopt the new philosophy. | Company leaders must adopt and fully support the new philosophy of continuous improvement through the empowerment of front-line workers. Cynical application of the new philosophy, with the sole intent of improving the bottom line, destroys interpersonal trust, which is essential to success. | School leaders must adopt and fully support the new philosophy of continuous improvement through greater empowerment of teacher-student teams. Cynical application of the new philosophy, with the sole intent of improving district-wide test scores, destroys interpersonal trust which, is essential to success. |

# APPENDIX 3—*continued*

| POINT | COMPANIES | SCHOOLS |
|---|---|---|
| 3 Cease dependence on mass inspection. | Reliance on assessment of the final product at the end of the production line is inherently wasteful. Substandard products must be trashed and replaced, or reworked to specifications. The right time for assessment is at every point in the entire production process. The best people for assessment are the customers and the people who are on the front lines of production. | Reliance on tests as the major means of assessment of student production is inherently wasteful and often neither reliable nor authentic. It is too late at the end of the unit to assess students' progress if the goal is to maximize their productivity. Tests and other indicators of student learning should be given as diagnostic and prescriptive instruments throughout the learning process. Learning is best shown by students' performance, applying information and skills to real-life challenges. Students must be taught how to assess their own work and progress if they are to take ownership of their own educational processes. |
| 4 End the practice of doing business on price tag alone. | Work closely with suppliers to build relationships of trust and collaboration. Don't allow only suppliers' prices to determine your company's use of their materials and services. Work together to maximize efficiency and productivity. | Build relationships of trust and collaboration within the school, and between school and the community. Everyone's roles as supplier and customer must be recognized and honored. Work together whenever possible to maximize the potentials of students, teachers, administrators, and the community. |

# APPENDIX 3—*continued*

| POINT | COMPANIES | SCHOOLS |
|---|---|---|
| 5 Improve constantly and forever the system of production and service. | Company management must create and maintain the context in which the workers are empowered to make continuous progress in product and service improvement, while they minimize waste and inefficiency. | School administrators must create and maintain the context in which teachers are empowered to make continuous progress in the quality of their learning and other aspects of personal development, while they learn valuable lessons from (temporary) failures. |
| 6 Institute programs of training. | Company leaders must institute programs of training for new workers. Effective training programs show workers how to set goals, how to work more effectively, and how to assess the quality of their own work. | School leaders must institute programs of training for new employees unfamiliar with the specific culture and expectations of the school. Effective training programs show new teachers how to set goals, how to teach effectively, and how to assess the quality of their work with students. Teachers must also institute programs in which students learn how to set learning goals, how to be more effective in their school work, and how to assess the quality of their own work. Teachers should show students by attitude and actions what a good *learner* is all about. (Educators learn how to be educators from the modeling they receive as students.) |

# APPENDIX 3—*continued*

| POINT | COMPANIES | SCHOOLS |
|---|---|---|
| 7 Institute leadership. | Leading consists of working with others as coach and mentor so that the organizational context in which improvement is valued and encouraged can be maximized by front-line workers. Leading is helping, not threatening or punishing. | School leadership consists of working with teachers, parents, students, and members of the community as coach and mentor so that the organizational context in which all students' growth and improvement is valued and encouraged can be maximized by teachers and students, parents, and community members who support the common effort. Leading is helping, not threatening or punishing. |
| 8 Drive out fear. | Fear is counterproductive, especially in the long term. Fear breeds distrust, cynicism, divisiveness, apathy, and disaffection, all of which lead to declines in productivity. Institutional changes must reflect shared power, shared responsibilities, and shared rewards. | Fear is counterproductive in school as it is in the workplace. Fear is destructive of the school culture and everything good that is intended to take place within it. Institutional changes must reflect shared power, shared responsibilities, and shared rewards. |
| 9 Break down barriers between staff areas. | Company productivity is enhanced when departments view themselves as partners in progress, and work together to maximize their potentials. Create cross-departmental and multi-level quality teams to break down role and status barriers to productivity. | Teacher and student productivity is enhanced when departments combine talents to create more integrated opportunities for learning and discovery. Create cross-departmental and multi-level quality teams to break down role and status barriers to productivity. |

| POINT | COMPANIES | SCHOOLS |
|---|---|---|
| 10  Eliminate slogans, exhortations, and targets for the workforce. | Workers who are in charge of their own production will create slogans, exhortations, and targets that are more meaningful than those imposed from above, as long as power, responsibility, and rewards are equitably distributed. When company expectations are not met, fix the system instead of fixing blame on individuals. | Teachers, students, administrators, families, and community members may collectively arrive at slogans and exhortations to improve their work together, as long as power, responsibility, and rewards are equitably distributed. When educational goals are not met, fix the system instead of fixing blame on individuals. |
| 11  Eliminate numerical quotas. | Quotas are numerical symbols that do not reflect the quality of the productive process, the integrity and health of the system, or long-term indicators of successes and failures. In fact, "hitting the numbers" as a short-term bottom-line solution to worker or company challenges is often useless or counterproductive in the long run. | Assignments and tests that focus attention on numerical or letter symbols of learning and production often do not fully reflect the quality of student progress and performance. When the grade becomes the bottom-line product, short-term gains replace student investment in long-term learning, and this may prove counter-productive in the long run. |
| 12  Remove barriers to pride and joy of workmanship. | Workers generally want to do good work and feel pride in it. Companies must dedicate themselves to removing the systemic causes of worker failure through close collaborative efforts. | Teachers and students generally want to do good work and feel pride in it. Schools must dedicate themselves to removing the systemic causes of teacher and student failure through close collaborative efforts. |

# APPENDIX 3—*continued*

| POINT | COMPANIES | SCHOOLS |
|---|---|---|
| 13 Institute a vigorous program of education and retraining. | Company management and the entire workforce require continuous learning programs if the company is to be on the leading edge and maximize customer satisfaction. Company people benefit from encouragement to enrich their education by exploring ideas and interests beyond the boundaries of their professional and personal worlds. Administrators, teachers, and students require continuous learning programs if the school is to be on the leading edge and maximize customer satisfaction. | All of the school's people benefit from encouragement to enrich their education by exploring ideas and interests beyond the boundaries of their professional and personal worlds. |
| 14 Take action to accomplish the transformation. | Company people at all levels must put this new philosophy into action so it becomes imbedded into the deep structure and culture of the organization. Workers alone cannot put the plan into effect. Constant top-level dedication to full implementation must be supported by a critical mass of company people to implement the plan and make it stick. | School personnel at all levels (including students) must put this new philosophy into action so it becomes imbedded into the deep structure and culture of the school. Teachers and students alone cannot put the plan into effect. Constant top-level dedication to full implementation must be supported by a critical mass of school and community people to implement the plan and make it stick. |

# APPENDIX 4
## The Quality Paradigm Shift in Education:
## from Teaching and Testing
## To Continuous Learning and Improvement

**OLD PARADIGM OF TEACHING AND TESTING**

**NEW PARADIGM OF CONTINUOUS LEARNING AND IMPROVEMENT**

Success if artificially limited to a few "winners." All others are made to consider themselves and their work as mediocre or inferior.

Unlimited, continuous improvement and successes are the objectives of schooling.

Competition-based.

Cooperation-based.

Lessons are linear, consecutive segments of one-way communication.

Learning is like a spiral with energy directed toward continuous improvement.

Product-oriented; focused solely on results, without acknowledgment of their short term nature. Grades and rankings important in themselves.

Process-oriented. Goals are important, but the process of getting to getting to the goal is at are least as significant.

Life, including schooling, is only worthwhile if you reach goals. The process has little or no intrinsic merit.

Life is a journey, and has intrinsic merit if lived with a zest for life, love, and learning. A "yearning and learning" is most important of all.

The system and its processes matter, as long as the ends are achieved. long as the ends are achieved.

The integrity and health of the system must be maintained, or the system will be suboptimized, and will eventually fail.

Work is a task, not intended to bring joy to the worker.

Work should be challenging, meaningful, and invigorating.

School as a place where teaching is done to (at) students. Students are passive, teachers are active.

School as a place where teachers and students learn how to get better and better at the work they do together.

## OLD PARADIGM

Teachers are isolated from each other by time and space.

Administration is viewed as the teachers' natural adversary (perhaps even enemy).

Teachers are viewed as the students' natural adversaries (perhaps even enemy).

Tayloresque factory model: Rule by compliance, providing control, command. Authoritarian, hierarchical. Fear used as tool of power.

Centralized control over curriculum, teaching methods, length of class periods, school day, school year, and so on.

Single-discipline instruction.

External validation of truth and the one right answer for every question asked by teacher.

Testing as primary means of assessing results of the learning process.

Instruction is set up to generate (right) answers.

## NEW PARADIGM

Teachers work together on school time to build success with each other and with a manageable number of students in a cohort group.

Administrators are viewed as teammates and helpers in removing the obstacles to student and teacher successes.

Teachers are viewed as teammates and helpers in removing obstacles to continuous success.

New model: Rule by helping, vision and leadership, making it possible for teachers and students to take pride in their work together, and to have joy in the processes (including the products) of continuous improvement.

Site-based management of curriculum, methods, time considerations, and so on.

Multi- and cross-discipline learning.

External and internal truths discovered through student's and teacher's questioning together.

Testing, when appropriate, to help modify (improve) the teaching/learning process. Others: process portfolios, exhibitions, and so on.

Instruction is set up to generate better and better questions, followed by student inquiry into

| OLD PARADIGM | NEW PARADIGM |
|---|---|
| | some of the areas of those questions. Student performances demonstrate improved understanding of the nature of the questions and some of the ways they might be solved. |
| Teachers give information; students memorize it, then forget most of it. | Students learn from teachers, other students, community and other sources, and incorporate those learnings into their lives, applying their insights as appropriate to real-life challenges. |
| Parents as outsiders, often made to feel unwelcome, even if unintentionally. | Parents as partners, suppliers, suppliers and customers. They are an integral part of the student's progress from the very beginning through the end of the schooling process. |
| Businesses sometimes welcomed to "adopt" a school; kept at arm's length. | Businesses invited to become partners (secondary suppliers and customers) in the students' continuous progress, not for direct commercial gain. |
| People of the community members encouraged to take part in the life of the school, or in the education of the community's young people. Not encouraged to have pride in the community schools. | People of the community brought into the school and made welcome, encouraged to contribute time and talents to the betterment of their school and their community's children. |
| Ultimate goal: Students as products of the school. | Ultimate goal: Students as their own products, continuously improving, getting better and better, and helping others to do the same. |

# APPENDIX 5
## Sources of Additional Information

*BOOKS AND ARTICLES*
### The Gurus—Their Ideas and Biographies

Deming, W.E. (1986). *Out of the Crisis*. Cambridge, Mass.: MIT Center for Advanced Engineering Study.

    The classic work on general principles of continuous improvement through statistical process control. The Deming "bible, including his famous Fourteen Points.

Deming, W.E. (1990). "System of Profound Knowledge." Unpublished monograph.

    Explains the four elements that are crucial to the success of any quality journey: appreciation for a system, some knowledge of the theory of variation, a theory of knowledge, and an understanding of human psychology.

Deming, W.E. (1992). *The New Economics for Industry, Education, Government*. Cambridge, Mass.: MIT Center for Advanced Engineering Study.

    A further examination of Deming's philosophy and its implications for these three sectors and America's future.

Feigenbaum, A. (1961). *Total Quality Control*. New York: McGraw-Hill.

    Industrial applications of Feigenbaum's Total Quality philosophy and practice.

Gabor, A. (1990). *The Man Who Discovered Quality: How W. Edwards Deming Brought the Quality Revolution to America*. N.Y.: Penguin Books.

    Detailed biography of Deming by an ardent admirer. Includes detailed accounts of TQM processes at Ford, Xerox, and General Motors.

Ishikawa, K. (1985). *What Is Quality Control? The Japanese Way*. Englewood Cliffs, N.J.: Prentice Hall.

    English translation of the late quality expert's introduction to Japanese quality control concepts and procedures, with rather muted references to Deming and Juran.

Juran, J.M. (1988). *Juran on Planning for Quality*. N.Y.: The Free Press.

    An in-depth description of Juran's Quality Trilogy®—quality

planning, quality control, and quality improvement, particularly as applied in industry.

Juran, J.M. (1989). *Juran on Leadership for Quality: An Executive Handbook.* N.Y.: The Free Press.

An extension of the concepts and practices detailed in Juran's 1988 work.

Kilian, C. (1992). *The World of W. Edwards Deming.* Knoxville, Tenn.: SPC Press.

An intimate look inside Deming's life and work by his longtime secretary and assistant.

Walton, M. (1991). *Deming Management at Work.* N.Y.: Perigee/Putnam.

Highly readable account of Deming's life and work. Explanations of Deming's Fourteen Points and "seven helpful charts"—otherwise known as the Seven Traditional Tools of TQM.

Walton, M. (1986). *The Deming Management Method.* N.Y.: Perigee/Putnam.

A brief recap of Deming's teachings, followed by detailed accounts of how his philosophy was applied (successfully) in five instances. Chapter 9, "Lessons Learned," is brief and instructive for all who seek to lead an organizational Quality movement.

### Basic TQM Concepts and Practices

Brassard, M. (1989) *The Memory Jogger Plus.* Methuen, Mass.: GOAL/QPC.

A handy little book showing the tools of TQM and examples of how they can be used.

Crosby, P.B. (1980). *Quality Is Free: The Art of Making Quality Certain.* N.Y.: Mentor/Penguin.

Explains that quality, in the long run, is cost-effective because quality is built into every process from the very beginning. "Zero defects" means savings.

Dobyns, L., and C. Crawford-Mason. (1991). *Quality or Else: The Revolution in World Business.* Boston: Houghton Mifflin.

Companion volume for the three-part PBS series. Includes a small section on the well-known Sitka experiment.

Garvin, D.A. (1988). *Managing Quality: The Strategic and Competitive Edge.* N.Y.: The Free Press.

In-depth look at the quality movement in industry, including the early impact of Deming, Juran, and others on the Japanese "miracle."

Hunt, V.D. (1992). *Quality in America: How to Implement a Competitive Quality Program*. Homewood, Ill.: Business One Irwin.

One of the most accessible introductions to TQM ideas applied to the improvement of business organizations. Applications to education are easy for readers to draw. Includes self-scoring inventories, tools and techniques of TQM, and a wealth of other information.

Imai, M. (1986). *Kaizen: The Key to Japan's Competitive Success*. N.Y.: McGraw Hill.

Wonderfully readable introduction to the concept of kaizen—the continuous incremental improvement process. Clearly presents applications to schools and other spheres of life.

Lareau, W. (1991). *American Samurai*. N.Y.: Warner.

Twenty "codas" or principles introduce readers to the thinking behind the Quality movement. Although focused on business, educational correlates are rather easy to draw.

Sashkin, M. and K.J. Kiser. (1993). *Putting Total Quality Management to Work*. San Francisco: Berrett-Koehler.

A brief and clearly written introduction to TQM focusing on tools, customers, and culture, with attention to first steps in implementing TQM.

## TQM Tools and Techniques

Kume, H. (1985). *Statistical Methods for Quality Improvement*. Tokyo: Association for Overseas Technical Scholarship.

Industrial applications for statistical analysis of quality processes. Advanced reading.

Mizuno, S., ed. (1988). *Management For Quality Improvement*. Cambridge, Mass.: Productivity Press.

Seven "new tools" for TQM application, primarily in industry. Advanced reading.

Ozeki, K., and T. Asaka. (1990). *Handbook of Quality Tools: The Japanese Approach*. Cambridge, Mass.: Productivity Press.

Step-by-step instructions for the use of TQM tools in industry. With a little work, these directions can be interpreted for education.

Scholtes, P.R., et al. (1988). *The Team Handbook*. Madison, Wis.: Joiner Associates.

How TQM ideas and tools can be used to build effective work teams, and a lot more. Oriented toward business, but highly adaptable to the work of educators.

### Educational Innovation

Bailey, E., D.L. Bayless, et al. (N.D.). "The Quality Improvement Management Approach As Implemented in a Middle School." Unpublished manuscript. Rockville, Md.: Westat Inc.

How Deming's Fourteen Points and the Seven Traditional Tools of TQM can help revitalize a middle school.

Berman, L. (1968). *New Priorities in the Curriculum*. Columbus: Charles E. Merrill.

A classic. Particularly interesting is Chapter 1, "Toward Process-Oriented Persons," in which the author urges a "thinking-feeling cohesion" in the development of curriculums and methodologies.

Berman, L., et al. (1991). *Toward Curriculum for Being*. Albany, N.Y.: State University of New York Press.

Transcript of five educators' ongoing dialogue about their own personal and professional journeys—their "curriculum for being."

Bonstingl, J.J. (1991). *Introduction to the Social Sciences*. Third edition.Englewood Cliffs, N.J.: Prentice Hall.

Middle school/high school survey course in the seven social sciences, with units on thinking and study skills development. Wrap-up unit focuses on students' options for the future, teaching them how to benefit from S-Teams and several of the new TQM tools described in *Schools of Quality*.

Bonstingl, J.J. (March 1992). "The Total Quality Classroom." *Educational Leadership* 49, 6: 67.

Basic ideas of TQM, its history and possible application to education.

Bonstingl, J.J. (November 1992). "The Quality Revolution in Education." *Educational Leadership* 49, 3.

Discusses how the Quality movement is beginning to sweep America, with vignettes of schools here and abroad where Quality principles are being put into practice. The Four Pillars of Total Quality organizations are described and applied to the work of schools.

Arató, L. (1992). "The World of Work and the World of School: An Interview With John Jay Bonstingl." Original title: "A munka vil_ga s az iskola vil_ga: Interj_ J.J. Bonstingl-lel. *Iskolakult_ra [School Culture], Journal of the Hungarian Institute of Public Education*, Budapest.

Conversation with the author, conducted by L_szl_ Arat_of the Hungarian Institute of Public Education, on the topic of TQM and its application to schools in their preparation of young people for the global workplace. English translation by Emese Dud_s and Erik Csupor, available from the author.

Brown, G.I., ed. (1975). *The Live Classroom: Innovation Through Confluent Education and Gestalt.* N.Y.: Viking.

An exploration of confluent learning in the classroom—linking students' hearts, heads, and hands to maximize the potentials for learning processes and outcomes.

Brown, R.G. (1991). *Schools of Thought.* San Francisco, Calif.: Jossey-Bass.

Suggests that we create schools where people learn how to be "thoughtful"—in both senses of the term. Particularly useful are the tables at the book's end, guidelines for program review from the Ontario Ministry of Education on issues concerning evaluation of learning processes and outcomes.

Fiske, E.B. (1991). *Smart Schools, Smart Kids: Why Do Some Schools Work?* N.Y.: Simon & Schuster.

A tour of several innovative American schools, with useful insights into the reasons for their successes.

Garlington, J., and A.T. Henderson. (1992). *Taking Stock: The Inventory of Family, Community, and School Support for School Achievement.* Washington, D.C.: National Committee for Citizens in Education.

Inventories for families and school personnel to assess the quality and health of a school's total support system.

Gardner, H. (1985). *Frames of Mind: The Theory of Multiple Intelligences.* N.Y.: Basic Books.

Gardner's theory of multiple intelligences. Argues that schools have traditionally cultivated a vary narrow spectrum of talents in young people, and proposes remedies.

Glasser, W. (1990). *The Quality School*. N.Y.: Harper & Row.

Glasser's interpretation of "control theory" as applied to Deming's teachings and school reform.

Goleman, D., P. Kaufman, and M. Ray. (1992). *The Creative Spirit*. N.Y.: Dutton/Penguin.

Companion volume for the PBS series. Particularly relevant are Chapter 2 "Creativity in Children" and Chapter 4 "Creating Community," which include Howard Gardner's theory of multiple intelligences and a visit to an Italian school where parents are fully involved in the children's joy-filled work at school.

Hansen, B.J., and C.L. Marburger. (1988). *School Based Improvement: A Manual for District Leaders*. Washington, D.C.: National Committee for Citizens in Education.

Provides ideas for getting everyone involved in your site-based continuous improvement process from the very beginning.

Hansen, B.J., and C.L. Marburger. (1989). *School Based Improvement: A Manual for Training School Councils*. Washington, D.C.: National Committee for Citizens in Education.

Explains how to train your school governing council for effective interaction and continuous improvement.

Henderson, A.T., C.L. Marburger, and T. Ooms. (1987). *Beyond the Bake Sale: An Educator's Guide to Working With Parents*. Washington, D.C.: National Committee for Citizens in Education.

Explains how to form positive relationships between educators and parents before a crisis occurs.

Henderson, A.T., and C.L. Marburger. (1990). *A Workbook on Parent Involvement for District Leaders*. Washington, D.C.: National Committee for Citizens in Education.

Describes ways to build effective parent involvement into school-based improvement.

Hewlett, S.A. (1991). *When the Bough Breaks: The Cost of Neglecting Our Children*. N.Y.: Basic Books.

Provides a wealth of background information on the societal impact of child neglect in America, with the author's proposed action plan for remediation. A glimpse of what happens to some children during the 91 percent of their lives when they are not in school.

*An Introduction to Total Quality for Schools.* (1991). Arlington, Va.: American Association of School Administrators.

Collection of articles about TQM and its applications to business and education.

*The Koalaty Kid Manual.* (1991). Milwaukee, Wis.: American Society for Quality Control.

Presents the basics for schools participating in the Koalaty Kid project.

Marburger, C.L. (1985). *One School at a Time: School Based Management—A Process for Change.* Washington, D.C.: National Committee for Citizens in Education.

Tells how schools can improve through shared decision making based upon mutual trust and interdependence.

Marzano, R.J. (1992). *A Different Kind of Classroom: Teaching with Dimensions of Learning.* Alexandria, Va.: Association for Supervision and Curriculum Development.

Introduction to the Dimensions of Learning program, which is useful in creating classroom interaction highly compatible with the TQM philosophy.

Melvin, C.A., III. (Summer 1991). "Restructuring Schools by Applying Deming's Management Theories." *Journal of Staff Development* 12, 3.

A superintendent's view of Deming's teachings and their application to the work of schools.

Neuroth, J., et al. (1992). *TQM Handbook.* Arlington, Va.: American Association of School Administrators.

Applies The Baldrige Award criteria to schools.

Olson, L. (May/June 1992). "Quality is Job One." *Teacher Magazine.*

Discusses how a few schools are applying Deming's teachings. Also in the same issue: "Changing Schools and Classrooms," a synopsis of current reform programs and concepts including cooperative learning, multiple intelligences, and whole language.

*Resource Guide for Total Quality Management in Texas Schools.* (1992). Austin, Tex.: Texas Association of School Administrators.

Provides basic information about TQM in education for administrators and teachers.

Rhodes, L.A. (November 1990). "Why Quality is Within Our Grasp . . . If We Reach." *The School Administrator*, p. 31.

Essential Deming teachings applied to school improvement. Part 1 of a 2-part series.

Rhodes, L.A. (December 1990). "Beyond Your Beliefs: Quantum Leaps Toward Quality Schools." *The School Administrator*, p. 23.

Answers the question: What is "the Deming superintendent" and what does he or she do? Part 2 of a 2-part series.

Rich, D. (1992). *MegaSkills: How Families Help Children Succeed in School and Beyond.* Boston: Houghton Mifflin.

Second edition of a classic about how parents and family members can support their children in schoolwork through greater interaction.

Schargel, F.P. (November/December 1991). "Promoting Quality in Education." *Vocational Education Journal*, p. 34.

Administrator tells how Quality principles were successfully applied at New York City's largest vo-tech school.

Schlechty, P.C. (1991). *Schools for the Twenty-First Century: Leadership Imperatives for Educational Reform.* San Francisco, Calif.: Jossey-Bass.

A good analysis of the systemic nature of successful school improvement processes.

Schlechty, P., and B. Cole. (Winter 1991) "Creating a System that Supports Change." *Educational Horizons*, p. 78.

Tells how stakeholders can be helped to create support systems that promote positive change.

Solomon, R.D., and E.C. Lanter Solomon. (1987). *The Handbook for the Fourth R: Volume I—Relationship Skills; Volume II-Relationship Skills for Group Discussion and Process.* Columbia, Md.: National Institute for Relationship Training.

Practical training in interpersonal relationship skills through activities.

Solomon, R.D., N. Davidson, and E.C. Lanter Solomon. (1994). *The Handbook for the Fourth R: Volume III—Relationship*

Activities for Cooperative and Collegial Learning. Columbia, Md.: National Institute for Relationship Training, Inc. An interpersonal relationship training program for professionals.

Stampen, J.O. (1987). "Improving the Quality of Education: W. Edwards Deming and Effective Schools." *Contemporary Education Review* 3, 3: 423.

Examination of linkages between Deming's teachings and effective schools research.

Stanko, J.A. (1991). "A Descriptive Study of the Metodo Natural e Integral as Applied at the Centro de Educacion Natural e Integral Montevideo, Uruguay." Unpublished master's thesis.

An intimate look at how CENI applies continuous improvement and "spiral learning" in this highly successful experimental Uruguayan elementary school.

Wiggins, G. (February 1991). "Standards, Not Standardization: Evoking Quality Student Work." *Educational Leadership* 48, 5: 18.

The importance of setting high-quality standards for students to work toward.

Wood, G.H. (1992). *Schools that Work: America's Most Innovative Public Education Programs.* N.Y.: Dutton/Penguin.

Describes schools where community involvement is the key to continuous improvement.

### Related Philosophies and Practices

Barker, J.A. (1992). *Future Edge: Discovering the New Paradigms of Success.* N.Y.: William Morrow.

Discusses the significance of paradigms and paradigm shifts in creating contexts for success and improvement.

Beale, L., and R. Fields. (1987). *The Win/Win Way.* San Diego, Calif.: Harcourt Brace Jovanovich.

Practical and inspirational insights into ways of setting up environments where everyone can succeed and improve.

Clarke, A.C. (1986). *July 20, 2019: Life in the 21st Century.* N.Y.: Omni/Macmillan.

Science fiction writer's view of daily life in the next century. Chapter 5, "School Days: No Recess," is a compelling look at the gap educators must bridge between past and present realities and the requirements of the future.

Covey, S.R. (1991). *Principle-Centered Leadership.* N.Y.: Summit Books.

Effective leadership is based upon adherence to natural principles and an unwavering focus on total quality and continuous improvement. Chapter 31, "Principle-Centered Learning Environments," applies this concept to schools. Follow-up to his *7 Habits of Highly Effective People*.

Csikszentmihalyi, M. (1990). *Flow, The Psychology of Optimal Experience: Steps Toward Enhancing the Quality of Life*. N.Y.: Harper Perennial.
Improvement of the quality of one's life is inextricably connected with the quality of life in family, community, and work settings. Explains how to optimize the life experience through greater awareness.

De Pree, M. (1989). *Leadership Is an Art*. N.Y.: Doubleday.
Delightful essays on leadership for empowerment by the chairman of Herman Miller, an innovative furniture manufacturing company.

De Pree, M. (1992). *Leadership Jazz*. N.Y.: Doubleday Currency.
More on the topic of humane leadership, development of creativity in workers, and the importance of compassion in all facets of life.

Ferguson, M. (1980). *The Aquarian Conspiracy*. Boston: Houghton Mifflin.
A classic on the art of empowerment in the new paradigm of teaching and learning. Especially compelling is Chapter 9, "Flying and Seeing: New Ways to Learn."

Fromm, E. (1976). *To Have Or To Be?* N.Y.: Harper & Row.
A full treatment of the "having mode" and the "being mode" of existence. Chapter 2, "Having and Being in Daily Experience," applies this philosophy to learning, remembering, reading, and caring.

Kohn, A. (1986). *No Contest: The Case Against Competition*. Boston: Houghton Mifflin.
Why, according to the author, the rewards of working together are always greater than working in competition with each other.

Kuhn, T. S. (1970). *The Structure of Scientific Revolutions*. Chicago: University of Chicago Press.
The foundation for all subsequent discussions of paradigms and paradigm shifts.

Leonard, G. (1978). *The Silent Pulse*. N.Y.: E.P. Dutton.
Intriguing exploration of the ways humans are intrinsically connected within their own selves and with other humans.

Lewin, K. (1948). *Resolving Social Conflicts*. New York: Harper.

The Force Field, now widely used as a TQM tool, was first developed in this work.

Marshall, R. and M. Tucker. (1992). *Thinking for a Living: Work, Skills, and the Future of the American Economy*. New York: Basic Books.

American education today reflects the factory model of the Industrial Revolution. The authors describe the changes necessary if schools are to prepare young people for the global working world of the future.

Nair, K. (1990). *Beyond Winning: The Handbook for the Leadership Revolution*. Phoenix: Paradox Press.

Essential principles for building win/win environments.

Orsborn, C. (1992). *Inner Excellence*. San Rafael, Calif.: New World Library.

Seven principles for reclaiming quality in your personal and professional life.

Rogers, C. (1980). *A Way of Being*. Boston: Houghton Mifflin.

How to build person-centered communities, schools, and businesses. "The Process of Education and Its Future" speaks to the need for heartful schools if we are serious about maximizing the potentials of young people.

Sashkin, M. and R.L. Williams. (1990). "Does Fairness Make a Difference?" *Organizational Dynamics*, 19, 2, pp. 56-71.

Research shows that workers' perceptions of 9 aspects of fairness in the workplace impact directly the organization's productivity, absentee rates, and the physical and mental health of employees.

Schlossstein, (1989). *The End of the American Century*. N.Y.: Congdon and Weed.

Explores what went wrong with America and how we can make it right. Part 3, "The Legacy of Confucius: Forging Educational Excellence," sheds light on social and educational issues from a multinational perspective.

Von Oech, R. (1983). *A Whack on the Side of the Head*. N.Y.: Warner Books.

A highly entertaining workbook for those who want to explore their own creative capabilities beyond the "one right answer." Tells how to open the 10 "mental locks" blocking your natural creativity.

Von Oech, R. (1986). *A Kick in the Seat of the Pants*. N.Y.: Perennial Library/Harper & Row, Publishers.

Another entertaining workbook on developing creativity in yourself and others through the "four roles of the creative process: the explorer, the artist, the judge, and the warrior."

Wellins, R.S., W.C. Byham, and J.M. Wilson. (1991). *Empowered Teams: Creating Self-Directed Work Groups That Improve Quality, Productivity, and Participation*. San Francisco, Calif.: Jossey-Bass.

Explains how to build strong, interactive, effective teams from the ground up.

### Business Perspectives

Altany, D. (November 5, 1990). "Copycats." *Industry Week*, pg. 11.

A good introduction to the use of benchmarking in businesses' continuous improvement processes. Copying isn't cheating anymore!

*America's Choice: High Skills or Low Wages!* (1990). Rochester, N.Y.: National Center on Education and the Economy.

Landmark document citing an action plan for business and education to use to improve the workforce of tomorrow.

Block, P. (1991) . *The Empowered Manager: Positive Political Skills at Work*. San Francisco, Calif.: Jossey-Bass.

A warm and insightful look at how managers can best empower themselves and all other people in the organization.

*Blueprint for Business on Restructuring Education*. (1989). Washington, D.C.: National Alliance of Business.

A guidebook for businesses to build "comfort zones" and mutual support projects with schools.

Bowles, J., and J. Hammond. (1991). *Beyond Quality: How 50 Winning Companies Use Continuous Improvement*. N.Y.: G.P. Putnam's Sons.

The title says it all. Its three appendixes summarize the Baldrige Award criteria, the ideas of the TQM pioneers, and the guidelines for a national government quality award.

Bradford, D.L., and A.R. Cohen. (1984). *Managing for Excellence: The Guide to Developing Hiqh Performance in Contemporary Organizations*. N.Y.: John Wiley and Sons.

Explains how managers can develop a successful learning organization through team-building.

Halberstam, D. (1986). *The Reckoning.* N.Y.: William Morrow. Extensive history of American automobile industry' s rise, fall, and attempted resurrection.

Especially interesting: Chapter 17, "Deming Finds An Audience"—an account of Deming's early work with Japan's carmakers.

Howard, V.A., and J.H. Barton. (1992). *Thinking Together: Making Meetings Work.* N.Y.: William Morrow.

Designed for companies, these insights are equally valuable for educators who want to use their limited time together most productively.

Johnson, W.B., and A.E. Packer. (1987). *Workforce 2000: Work and Workers for the Twenty-First Century.* Indianapolis, Ind.: Hudson Institute.

Essential data for understanding America's shifting demographics and what they mean for education.

Kolberg, W.H., and F.C. Smith. (1992). *Rebuilding America's Workforce.* Homewood, Ill.: Business One Irwin.

Detailed examination of America' s declining productivity with prescriptions for educators, families, businesses, and communities. See especially Chapter 8: " Closing the Education Gap."

*Learning a Living: A Blueprint for High Performance—A SCANS Report for America 2000. (1992).* Washington, D.C.: U.S. Department of Labor.

Follow-up to *What Work Requires of Schools.* Explains the basic workplace skills young people should have for success.

Lynch, R.F. (April 1991). "Shedding the Shackles of George Patton, Henry Ford, and First-Grade Teachers." *Quality Progress,* pg. 63.

What American education must consider in its examination of Taylorism.

Nykiel, R.A. (1992). *You Can't Lose If the Customer Wins.* Stamford, Conn.: Longmeadow Press.

A primer on customer-supplier relations and business success.

Ohmae, K. (1990). *The Borderless World: Power and Strategy in the Interlinked Economy.* N.Y.: Harper Business.

A look at the importance of quality in the emerging global marketplace.

Petersen, D.E., and J. Hillkirk. (1991). *A Better Idea: Redefining the Way Americans Work.* Boston: Houghton Mifflin.

How Ford Motor Company turned itself around, making quality every employee's "Job 1."

Roddick, A. (1991). *Body and Soul: Profits with Principles.* N.Y.: Crown Publishers.

The key to success is for company management to establish environments in which workers' creativity is unleashed and their potentials are maximized. By the founder of the Body Shop chain of stores.

Rosenbluth, H.F., and D.M. Peters. (1992). *The Customer Comes Second.* N.Y.: William Morrow.

Who comes first? Your workers do! The way you treat your workers is the way they treat customers. Implications for school administrators?

Senge, P.M. (1990a). *The Fifth Discipline: The Art and Practice of the Learning Organization.* N.Y.: Doubleday Currency.

Businesses and other organizations must become "learning organizations" that discover how to promote learning if they are to survive and thrive.

Senge, P.M. (Fall 1990). "The Leader's New Work: Building Learning Organizations." *Sloan Management Review* 31, 1: 7.

A good synthesis of *The Fifth Discipline.*

Townshend, P.L., and J.E. Gebhardt. (1990). *Commit To Quality.* N.Y.: John Wiley and Sons.

How the author, as CEO of an innovative insurance company, "talks the walk and walks the talk" of quality.

Townshend, P.L., and J.E. Gebhardt. (1992). *Quality in Action: 93 Lessons in Leadership, Participation, and Measurement.* N.Y.: John Wiley and Sons.

A wealth of insights into the creation and growth of quality organizations, with a few ideas specifically for education.

*What Work Requires of Schools: A SCANS Report for America 2000.* (1991). Washington, D.C.: U.S. Department of Labor.

Presents the basic competencies required of today's workers by business, with implications for schools, families, and communities.

**Audio and Video Materials**

*Assignment: Total Quality Management in Schools.* (1992). Columbia, Md.: The Center for Schools of Quality.

Audiotape conversation with John Jay Bonstingl, focusing on how his Four Pillars of Schools of Quality and Deming's Fourteen Points can reinvigorate schools, as they have done for many businesses.

*Educational Leadership on Tape.* (November 1992). Alexandria, Va.: Association for Supervision and Curriculum Development.

Audiotape renditions of articles in the journal's November 1992 issue, which focuses on TQM in education.

*Discovering the Future: The Business of Paradigms.* (1989). Burnsville, Minn.: Charthouse Learning Corporation.

Joel Barker introduces the concept of paradigms and illustrates their significance in preparing for change. Videotape and 16mm formats.

*Discovering the Future: The Power of Vision.* (1990). Burnsville, Minn.: Charthouse Learning Corporation.

Joel Barker explores the relationship between positive visions of the future and the development of creativity in individuals and organizations. Videotape and 16mm film formats.

*If Japan Can, Why Can't We?* (1980). Chicago: Films, Inc.

The original NBC TV documentary that introduced America to the work of Deming in Japan.

*Koalaty Kid: A Commitment to Quality in Elementary Education.* (1992). Milwaukee, Wis.: ASQC.

Eight-minute videotape overview of the Koalaty Kid project in action at Carder Elementary School in Corning, New York.

*Principle-Centered Leadership.* (1991). Provo, Utah: Covey Leadership Center.

Audiotape adaptation by Stephen Covey of the material in his book of the same title. Six tape set.

*Quality Or Else!* (1991). Chicago: Films, Inc.

Three-part PBS series on the TQM revolution in business and education, and why it is desperately needed. Videotape format.

*Quest for Quality.* (1991). Arlington, Va.: American Association of School Administrators.

Interviews with John Jay Bonstingl, Stephen Covey, William Glasser, and David Langford, and others on the topic of TQM applied to the work of schools. Two cassette audiotape set.

*W. Edwards Deming: Prophet of Quality.* (1992) Chicago: Films, Inc.

The life and work of Deming. Videotape format.

*The Deming Library.* Chicago: Films, Inc.

A 16-part videotape series in which W. Edwards Deming explains and demonstrates his philosophy.

## ORGANIZATIONS AND NETWORKS

TQM-Education Network of the Association for Supervision and Curriculum Development
Contact: John Jay Bonstingl
Facilitator
c/o The Center for Schools of Quality
P.O. Box 810
Columbia, MD 21044
(410) 997-7555

Grassroots network to share and learn about TQM innovations in education. Newsletter, membership list, and advance notice about conferences, seminars, and materials on TQM in schools. Annual fee: $10.

American Association of School Administrators
Quality Network
Contact: Martha J. Bozman
1801 North Moore Street
Arlington, VA 22209
(703) 528-0700

Newsletter, TQM articles, information about conferences, seminars, and products.

American Society for Quality Control
Contact: Barbara Shaw
Public Relations and Marketing
P.O. Box 3005
Milwaukee, WI 53201
(414) 765-7217 / 272-8575 / (800) 248-1946 outside Milwaukee

Membership organization of statistical quality control professionals. Institutional home of the worldwide Koalaty Kid project. Information, videotape about the project. Membership in ASQC includes *Quality Progress*, a monthly publication about quality issues.

The Center for Schools of Quality
John Jay Bonstingl
Director
P.O. Box 810
Columbia, MD 21044
(410) 997-7555

Instructional materials and training for school leaders, policy-makers, teachers, parents, businesses, and communities, focusing on the application of TQM principles and practices.

GOAL/QPC
Contact: Sue Tucker
Director of Education Policy
13 Branch Street
Methuen, MA 01844
(508) 685-3900

Nonprofit TQM research and publishing organization.

Home and School Institute, Inc.
Contact: Dorothy Rich
President
1201 Sixteenth Street, N.W.
Washington, DC 20036
(202) 466-3633

Innovative programs for families and teachers working together to nurture children's achievement in the school, at home, and in the community.

National Committee for Citizens in Education
Contact: Chrissie Bamber
Assistant Executive Director
900 Second Street, N.E., Suite 8
Washington, DC 20002
(202) 408-0447

Books and training in building effective relations between schools, parents, and the community.

National Institute for Relationship Training, Inc.
Contact: Richard D. Solomon
President
9240 Broken Timber Way
Columbia, MD 21045
(410) 730-5500
   Instructional materials and training for educators and students in active listening, team-building, and other essential skills.

World Center for Community Excellence
Contact: William M. DeCrease
Director
1006 State Street
Erie, PA 16501
(814) 456-9223
   Helps communities create and develop their own community quality councils throughout the United States and around the world.

# References

Barker, J.A. (1992). *Future Edge*. New York: Morrow, p. 31.

Bayless, D.L., G. Massaro, et. al. (1992). "SouthEastern Regional Vision for Education: Quality Improvement." Unpublished document, p. 80.

Berman, L.M. (1968). *New Priorities in the Curriculum*. Columbus: Merrill, p. 9.

Bonstingl, J.J. (1991). *Introduction to the Social Sciences*. Englewood Cliffs, N.J.: Prentice Hall, pp. 8-10.

Bonstingl, J.J. (March 1992). "The Total Quality Classroom." *Educational Leadership* 49, 6: 67.

Brown, G.I. (1975). *The Live Classroom: Innovation Through Confluent Education and Gestalt*. New York: The Viking Press.

Clarke, A.C. (1986). *July 20, 2019: Life in the 21st Century*. New York: Omni/Macmillan, p. 76.

Crosby, P. (1980). *Quality is Free: The Art of Making Quality Certain*. New York: Mentor/Penguin.

Deming, W.E. January 23-24, 1992. Seminar.

Ferguson, M. (1980). *The Aquarian Conspiracy*. Los Angeles, Calif.: Tarcher, p. 228.

Fromm, E. (1976). *To Have Or To Be?* New York: Harper & Row. p. 29, 77-78.

Gabor, A. (1990). *The Man Who Discovered Quality*. New York: Penguin, p. 77.

Garvin, D.A. (1988). *Managing Quality*. New York: The Free Press, pp. 180-4.

Gottlieb, D. (January 15, 1984). *The Washington Post*, page D-3.

Halberstam, D. (1986). *The Reckoning*. New York: Morrow, p. 314-5.

Henderson, A.T., C.L. Marburger, and T. Ooms. (1987). *Beyond the Bake Sale: An Educator's Guide to Working with Parents*. Washington, D.C.: National Committee for Citizens in Education.

Ishikawa, K. (1985). *What Is Total Quality Control? The Japanese Way*. Englewood Cliffs, N.J.: Prentice Hall, pp. 25-8.

Juran, J.M. (1988). *Juran on Planning for Quality*. New York: The Free Press, pp. 6-15.

Kilian, C. (1992). *The World of W. Edwards Deming*. Knoxville, Tennessee: SPC Press, p. 174.

*Koalaty Kid Manual*. (1991). Milwaukee, Wis.: American Society for Quality Control, p. ii.

Leonard, G. (1978). *The Silent Pulse*. New York: Dutton, p. 41.

Lewin, K. (1948). *Resolving Social Conflicts*. New York: Harper.

Lynch, R.F. (April 1991). "Shedding the Shackles of George Patton, Henry Ford, and First-Grade Teachers." *Quality Progress* p. 64.

Marshall, R. and M. Tucker. (1992) *Thinking for a Living: Work, Skills, and the Future of the American Economy*, New York: Basic Books, p. 17.

"The Quality Revolution" (1989). Film broadcast on PBS, Dystar Television.

Sashkin, M., and K.J. Kiser. (1983) *Putting Total Quality Management to Work.* San Francisco, Calif.: Berrett-Koehler Publishers.

Senge, P.M. (1990). *The Fifth Discipline.* New York: Doubleday, p. 4.

Scholtes, P.R. (1988). *The Team Handbook.* Madison, Wis.: Joiner Associates, pp. 2-18 to 2-21.

Stanko, J.A. (1968). "A Descriptive Study of the Metodo Natural e Integral as Applied at the Centro de Educacion Natural e Integral Montevideo, Uruguay." Unpublished Master's Thesis, p. 68.

Taba, H., et al. (1971). *A Teacher's Handbook to elementary Social Studies: An Inductive Approach.* Reading, Mass.: Addison-Wesley Publishing Company.

von Oech, R. (1983). *A Whack on the Side of the Head.* New York: Warner, p. 21.

Walton, M. (1991). *Deming Management at Work.* New York: Perigee/Putnam, p. 16.

Walton, M. *The Deming Management Method.* (1986). New York: Perigee/Putnam, p. 13.

# Acknowledgments

I am indebted to a great many people for helping me think through the concepts of TQM and supporting my efforts in a wide variety of ways.

I would like, first and foremost, to thank W. Edwards Deming for his pioneering work in this field, and for taking time to share his invaluable insights with me. My appreciation also to Ceil Kilian, his longtime assistant, for her many kindnesses.

My appreciation also goes to: David Bayless, Nancy Bayless, and Gabriel Massaro, Bayless & Associates; Michael J. Clark, independent journalist; Clare Crawford-Mason, Robert Mason, and Scott Stein, CC-M Productions; Lorraine Flowers, Maryland State Department of Education; Barry Gomberg, Weber State College; Anne Gurvin, U.S. Information Agency; Julie Horine, University of Mississippi; Barbara Hummell, Madison Area Quality Improvement Network; Ed Janus, Corporate Radio Network; Don McCain, World Center for Community Excellence; Barbara McCormick, Office of Texas Governor Ann Richards; Jay McTighe, Maryland Assessment Consortium; Carl Marburger and Barbara Hansen, consultants in school-community relations; Tom Mosgaller, City of Madison, Wisconsin; Jan Partain, Arkansas Industrial Development Committee; Yvonne Thayer, Virginia State Department of Education; Marshall Sashkin, OERI, U.S. Department of Education; Karen Schriver, Carnegie Mellon University; Peggy Siegel, Sandra Byrne, Patricia Mitchell, National Alliance of Business; Ronald Pahl, California State University, Fullerton; Lewis Rhodes, Martha Bozman, and Judy Nash, American Association of School Administrators; Pam Sheehan, World Affairs Council of Pittsburgh; Fred Shemanek, North Central Deming Management Forum; Jim Sheridan, The Olive Branch Restaurant; and Jeannette Stanko, University of Maryland, Baltimore County.

Thanks also to my international friends and colleagues for their bountiful assistance: Hon. Shinichiro Horie, Embassy of Japan; Professor Shinichi Suzuki, Waseda University Tokyo; Professor Jost Reischmann, University of Tübingen, Germany; Professor Shi Weiping, East China Normal University; Deputy State Secretary for Education Dobos Krisztina, and Tibor Bognar, László Arató, Ildiko Polgar, Maria Guoth, and Professors Beáta Kochy and Ivan Falus of Eötvös Loránd University, Budapest, Hungary; and Professors Unni Hagen and Ellen Carm, University of Oslo, Norway.

My thanks to the school leaders who shared ideas and insights on TQM with me over the years: Kenneth Arndt, Elyria, Ohio; Diane Barker,

Virginia Beach, Virginia; Spicer Bell, Cambridge, Maryland; Den Boyd, Prince William County, Virginia; Robert Bender, Meadville, Pennsylvania; Albertha Caldwell, Glenwood, Maryland; Phyllis Cohen, Nelson Diaz, Merri Mann, and Janet McAliley, Miami, Florida; Robert D. Conn, Holden, Massachusetts; Thomas Conner, Washington, Pennsylvania; Bonnie Daniel, Columbia, Maryland; David Gangel, Rappahannock County, Virginia; Constance Goldman, Cape Elizabeth, Maine; Debby Gomberg, Provo, Utah; Robert Gratz, Belvedere, New Jersey; Terry Grier, Akron, Ohio; Thomas Houlihan, Johnston County, North Carolina; Lee Jenkins, Redding, California; Christine Jensen, Anchorage, Alaska; Thomas Labanc, Upper St. Clair, Pennsylvania; Paul Longhofer, Wichita, Kansas; Larry Macaluso, Red Lion, Pennsylvania; Charles Melvin, Beloit-Turner, Wisconsin; Harrell G. Miller, Napa, California; Randee Reisinger, Waco, Texas; Larrae Rocheleau, Sitka, Alaska; Charles Slemenda, Tarboro, North Carolina; Len Strnad, Elyria, Ohio; William Switala, Bethel Park, Pennsylvania; Richard Ten Haken, Spencerport, New York; Guy Vander Vliet, Piscataway, New Jersey;

John Vanko, St. Charles, Illinois; Thomas E. Walsh, Casper, Wyoming; and Richard Weeter, Oklahoma City, Oklahoma.

Most of all, I am eternally grateful to my family: my mother Catherine, late father Joseph, aunt Madalene Taucher, late uncles Pete and Herman, and aunt and uncle Ann and Joseph Neville for their constant loving support throughout the years and for providing me with my first lessons in quality. My deepest appreciation also to my students, past and present; they have been some of my very best teachers.

There are many others whose significant contributions are not recognized here due to the failure of memory, and I beg their forgiveness. Please know that their ideas have helped greatly.

Of course, all of the ideas expressed here are ultimately my sole responsibility, and they should not be construed as reflecting the beliefs of the many people who helped bring this book to fruition.

J.J.B.

# About the Author

John Jay Bonstingl is an international education consultant special-
izing in the application of Total Quality Management concepts and
practices to the continuous improvement of schools as "learning organizations." He is founder and director of The Center for Schools of Quality,
an outreach effort to help schools, families, businesses, and communities
combine forces to bring Total Quality into the classroom. He may be
contacted at P.O. Box 810, Columbia, Maryland 21044, or by telephone
and fax at (410) 997-7555.

# Current ASCD Networks

ASCD sponsors numerous networks that help members exchange ideas, share common interests, identify and solve problems, grow professionally, and establish collegial relationships. The following networks may be of particular interest to readers of this book. For information about other networks, call ASCD's Field Services Department at (703) 549-9110, ext. 506.

### TQM - Education
*Contact:* John Jay Bonstingl, Consultant, P.O. Box 810, Columbia, Maryland 21044. Telephone: (410) 997-7555. FAX: (410) 997-7555.

### Quality Schools/OBE
*Contact:* Rick Scott, Chetwynd Secondary School, School District #59, P.O. Box 447, Chetwynd, B.C., Canada V0C 1J0. Telephone: (604) 788-2267.